THOMAS SHEPARD
PILGRIM FATHER AND
FOUNDER OF HARVARD

His Spiritual Experience and
Experimental Preaching

by
Alexander Whyte

REFORMATION HERITAGE BOOKS
Grand Rapids, Michigan

2007

Published by
Reformation Heritage Books
2965 Leonard St., NE
Grand Rapids, MI 49525
616-977-0599 / Fax 616-285-3246
e-mail: orders@heritagebooks.org
website: www.heritagebooks.org

This facsimile is taken from
Edinburgh and London:
Oliphant Anderson and Ferrier, 1909

ISBN 978-1-60178-008-9

CONTENTS

CONTENTS

THOMAS SHEPARD

I

INTRODUCTORY

HERE is natural religion and there is revealed religion, and there is national religion and there is family religion, and they are all good so far as they go. But the only soul-saving religion is the religion of a personal and a spiritual experience.

Thomas Shepard has been one of my favourite authors ever since the year 1861 when my honoured friend Dr. Williamson of Huntly wrote my name on his own copy of the Parable of the Ten Virgins. I think I must have read Shepard quite as often as Spurgeon had read Bunyan; quite as often at any rate as Jowett had read Boswell. And I am still reading Shepard as if I had never read him before. As a proof of that take this little confidence of mine. The week before my last short holiday I had read Professor Churton Collins's delightful paper on *The Tempest* that appeared in the *Contemporary Review* for the month of January last. And so impressed was I with the learned

Professor's paper that I took to the country with me Dr. Furness's variorum and monumental edition of that exquisite work, promising myself a great revel over the great text and over the rich mass of explanatory and illustrative notes. But would you believe it? with such a temptation lying on my table all the time I never once opened the seductive volume. For as God would have it, as John Bunyan was wont to say, I had taken Thomas Shepard also with me and I read the Parable, and the Sound Believer, and the Sincere Convert, and the Saint's Jewel, and the Select Cases, and the Spiritual Experiences over and over again; execrable English and all. And instead of repenting myself for my neglect of Shakespeare and his monumental editor, I came home thanking God again for His notable servant Shepard. And more than that, I came home more settled and resolved than ever to do all I can to make you know something of Shepard's matchlessly pungent lessons in spiritual and experimental religion. And I took out of my desk and read again to reassure me a postcard bearing the Aberdeen postmark, which I received some years ago and which runs thus: 'A thousand thanks for pressing Thomas Shepard on our attention. After long looking for it, I have at last got a copy of the Parable, and I can scarcely lay it down. It is proving itself a very book of life to me. This is the preaching that our day needs.—A FREE CHURCH MINISTER.'

I daresay you will remember that I was always

besieging you to buy and to read and to read all your days, as also to distribute, the *Pilgrim's Progress* and the *Grace Abounding*. But you will have perfect peace of mind concerning Thomas Shepard and his works. For I shall never ask one of you to spend one penny on Shepard, such is his atrocious English. Bunyan and Shepard are at one in the deepest things, but they stand at opposite poles in the matter of their English style. Shepard at his very best wrote an all but unrecognisable English. But after the New England printers and then the Aberdeen printers had put Shepard's best book through their hands, if hands they could be called, Shepard came forth absolutely unreadable, unless to a few resolved and relentless and irresistible readers, such as Mrs. Black of Dunnikier Manse, and Dr. Foote of Brechin, and Dr. Williamson, and myself. Much as I respect William Greenhill's judgment, I cannot follow him when he says of Shepard that ' here is a cornfield without cockle or thorns or thistles.' I know what Greenhill means when he says all that, and I wholly subscribe to his deep meaning. But if I were to repeat his words without some warning, you might be led into advertising for the old book which you would no sooner open than you would throw it down in disgust and in indignation both at Shepard and at Greenhill and at me. ' Polybius,' says Dr. Butcher, ' pays the penalty attaching to neglect of form ; he is read by few.' At the same time I will say this.

As we find Principal Rendall quite frankly acknowledging the heavy cramped vocabulary, and the deadness of expression, and the formless monotony of clause that all combine to weigh down the First Book of Marcus Aurelius: while at the same time he stands up against Matthew Arnold when that critic says that the Emperor's style lacks distinction and physiognomy, so will I stand up for Shepard's distinction and for his physiognomy. The truth is while repeating and exaggerating all the stoic Emperor's faults of style, Shepard's mental countenance is even more unmistakable to me than is that of the royal author of the immortal Thoughts. There is no possibility of our ever mistaking a page or a paragraph or even a sentence of Thomas Shepard's. Not only because of its unparalleled shapelessness but much more because of its Paul-like hands and feet. For Shepard, once he has got on your track, will follow hard after you all your days. And once he gets a real hold of you, you will never be able for long to shake him off again. But when all is said that can be said about Shepard's sluggard's-garden of a style, if you will go with me into the resolved study of this great Puritan I will promise you many a sweet and fragrant flower out of his crannied and crumbling walls, and many a medicinal herb out of his stoniest places, and many a cup of wine well refined out of his most gnarled or crabbed vinestocks. Just gird up your loins and come with me and see if it is not so. And as the saintly David Brainerd says, ' we shall see what passed for soul-saving religion with that so excellent and so venerable Pilgrim Father Thomas Shepard, the author of the *Sound Convert*, the *Spiritual Experiences*, and the *Parable Unfolded*.'

II

INTRODUCTORY : EVANGELICAL

AN excellent book was published the other day written by the Rev. Mr. Balleine, vicar of Bermondsey, and entitled *The Evangelical Party in the Church of England.* As I read that admirable book I resolved to carry out an intention I had often formed, that is to say, to devote a somewhat carefully prepared discourse to the true meaning and the rich contents and the personal applications of that well-known word 'Evangelical.'

And how rich are the contents and how manifold are the applications of the word Evangelical you may judge when I tell you that the word under discussion, with all its roots and with all its branches, occupies no less than seven folio columns of small print in Sir James Murray's great English Dictionary now in course of publication. Though Mr. Balleine confines his history to the Church of England he will have many delighted and thankful readers outside that Church. For the evangelical spirit is the only truly Catholic spirit—that is to say, it is the only spirit that rejoices in the success of the Gospel wheresoever and by whomsoever the Gospel is preached.

The Vicar of Bermondsey begins his book with an absolutely sickening chapter which he has entitled 'Before the Dawn'—that is to say, before the work of John Wesley and Charles Wesley and George Whitefield began in England. You would not believe to what a depth of heathenism England had sunk after the evangelical and spiritual life of puritanism had been extinguished in England. 'Before the Dawn' is an appalling chapter; but as it stands in Mr. Balleine's book it only serves the better to bring out the unspeakable blessing that the evangelical revival became to England, and not to England only but to the whole English-speaking world. After a rapid but brilliant sketch of the lives and labours of the two Wesleys and Whitefield the author passes on to give his readers a series of most delightful glimpses of the work of William Romaine, and John Thornton, and William Grimshaw, and Henry Venn, and Joseph Milner, and Thomas Adam, and Fletcher of Madeley, and Augustus Toplady, and James Hervey, and John Berridge, and John Newton, and William Cowper, and Thomas Scott, and Isaac Milner, and Charles Simeon, winding up with an excellent chapter on 'The Clapham Sect,' which 'sect,' so to call it, has been immortalised by Sir James Stephen in his fine essay. Altogether, Mr. Balleine's book is a great refreshment and a great encouragement to read; and it will do much to rehabilitate the evangelical party in the Church of England if that rehabilitation is anywhere really needed.

The original root of our well-known English word evangelical is laid open in the text. For evangelical is just transliterated Greek for 'good tidings of great joy.' The best way perhaps to bring out and set forth something of the depth and the riches and the manifold applications of this great word evangelical will be to give you some of the leading combinations into which this great word has entered in religious history and religious literature. To begin then at the very beginning: The word evangelical is as old as Eden itself. 'This,' says Coverdale, 'is the first sure evangel: this is the proto-evangel itself— that the seed of the woman is to come to bruise the serpent's head.' And ever since, wherever the seed of the woman is preached and is received and is rested on that is evangelical preaching, and that receiving and that resting on Him is evangelical and soul-saving faith. Without 'the seed of the woman' there is nothing that is truly evangelical anywhere. Whereas, on the other hand, with Him and with His redeeming and His sin-bruising work there always comes the good tidings of great joy to all the sad children of Adam and Eve.

The LORD GOD Himself was the first Evangelical Preacher and He found His first congregation hiding themselves from the presence of the LORD amongst the trees of the garden. And the LORD GOD having made a beginning He so loved and He so enjoyed, so to say, the evangelical office that He Himself took in hand to evangelise Abel, and Noah, and Abraham, and Isaac, and Jacob, and Joseph, and especially—Moses on the Mount, and still more especially David, as David sings in a hundred psalms. But the first time since Eden when this great name evangelical was given to any merely human preacher was when St. Jerome so designated the prophet Isaiah. As that old Latin Father worked his learned way through Isaiah rendering the ancient Hebrew into Vulgate Latin, he became so impressed with the number and the richness of the evangelical passages in that prophet that at last he said to himself, and actually wrote it down, that this wonderful man Isaiah should be reckoned as a New Testament evangelist rather than an Old Testament prophet. And it has been so ever since till Isaiah has been promoted to stand alongside of Matthew, and Mark, and Luke, and John themselves. Not that Jeremiah, and Ezekiel, and Hosea, and Micah are not evangelical, for they all are. But Isaiah has Jesus Christ so fully set forth in his prophetic pages that he has with universal acclamation received both the glorious name and the glorious place that he alone of all the Hebrew prophets holds. And it is the same when we come down to the Apostle Paul. Not that John, and James, and Peter, and the Epistle to the Hebrews are

not all richly evangelical; but Paul's own and
peculiar evangel, as he so proudly calls it, is the
pure and the full and the perfect and the final
evangel of them all. It is as an Egyptian Father
of the Desert has it: Matthew and Mark and
Luke and John supply the wool, but it is the
greatest of the apostles who alone weaves the
web and puts the dress upon us all so as to cover
all our nakedness, till we are able to say with
the prophet, 'I put on His righteousness and it
clothed me: it was to me for a robe and for a
diadem!'

And then from Paul and after Paul we get
what we call evangelical preaching.   'The
sermon,' says an able and clear-sighted writer,
'has ever been the great and central feature of
primitive and Protestant worship.'   'And,' he
continues, 'the sermon still serves to distinguish
the evangelical from the ritualistic type of Chris-
tianity.'   'The system called evangelical,' says
Sir James Stephen, 'is that system of which,
if Augustine, Luther, Calvin, Knox, and the
writers of the English Homilies are to be believed, Christ Himself was the Author, and Paul
the first and the greatest interpreter.'   And in a
truly noble note on Hooker, Coleridge argues
thus on this same subject—'Whose parishes
were the best disciplined, whose flocks were the
best fed, were the soberest livers, and were the
most awakened and best-informed Christians—
was it not those of the puritan and evangelical
preachers?   In whose churches and parishes

were all the other pastoral duties—catechising,
visiting the poor and the sick, and the like, most
strictly practised ? ' By universal admission
Samuel Taylor Coleridge is by far our best
writer on Shakespeare ; but for myself I like
him still better in his ' Notes on English Divines,'
and especially on Hooker.

Evangelical theologians is a special and a dis-
tinguishing designation that the true successors
of the apostle have always borne in the Church
of Christ. There was a fine series of Sabbath
evening lectures delivered in this pulpit five-and-
twenty years ago, and entitled, ' The Evangelical
Succession.' The special object of the lectures,
as the advertisement ran, was to exhibit the true
genius of the Evangelical Principle : to trace its
manifestation, development, and vicissitudes in
various ages of the Church and human history,
and to illustrate its ruling and moulding power
over diverse types of national, intellectual, and
spiritual character. As Dr. Rainy said in opening
the series, ' If there is a type of Christian doctrine
and life which can legitimately be distinguished
by this name evangelical, then no doubt that
type of doctrine and life looks back to the
Apostle Paul as among the apostolic circle its
very special forerunner. Evangelical dòctrine
and the evangelical life find, in his epistles and
in his spirit, some of their most significant
warrants and supports.' Some of the ablest
scholars and preachers of that day followed Dr.
Rainy's introductory lecture on Paul with such

evangelical successors of Paul as Augustine, and Anselm, and Luther, and Calvin, and Knox, and Rutherford, and Baxter, and Owen, and Bunyan, and Edwards, and Chalmers. For those great names unite to form a great evangelical chain which stretches down from apostolic days to our own day, thanks be to God!

After describing the dismal condition of public worship in the pre-Wesley days in England, Mr. Balleine goes on to say that ' the greatest change which the evangelicals made in public worship was the introduction of hymn-singing.' And you know yourselves what a change for the better has come in Scotland also with the spread of evangelical life and feeling in the matter of our public and private praise. Preserving the psalms and the paraphrases in their own proper place, who that has once entered into the evangelical enlargement that has come to our public worship and to our family worship with the great evangelical and experimental hymns would ever consent to forego that liberty and that enlargement and that enriching? How much do we in Scotland owe under God to the psalms and hymns and spiritual songs of Reformation times, and to the successive harvests of spiritual song that have been reaped out of every season of reformation and revival! What a new wealth of worship has come to us out of such evangelical hymns as Wesley's, and Newton's, and Cowper's, and Toplady's, and Bonar's, and many suchlike hymns of genius and of grace! Public worship with

ourselves in this house is a new thing, never to
be enough acknowledged, since the coming of
the great evangelical hymns, with those instru-
mental accompaniments and supports which we
so much enjoy, and to which we are so much
indebted.

And then, from all that, no one can surely
mistake what is meant when evangelical churches
are spoken of, and evangelical parties in non-
evangelical churches, such as the present Church
of England.   We come on this ecclesiastical
expression in *Waverley*, where Sir Walter says
of one of his characters, ' I have never been
able to discover whether he belonged to the
evangelical or to the moderate party in the kirk.'
On which passage it occurs to remark that had
Sir Walter belonged to the evangelical party himself, he would then have been in a position to
make the discovery that he is here in search of,
and to make that discovery infallibly and without
any doubt.   And more than that, Sir Walter
Scott would then have been a perfect portrayer
and universally accepted of our best Scottish life,
which, as things are, he is not, and never can be
accepted as being.

And then, from all that, we have evangelical
graces spoken of as belonging to the individual
believer—as for instance evangelical humility.   In
illustration take this classical passage out of
Jonathan Edwards, that majestic evangelical
himself, a passage which, simply to quote, could
I quote it all, would be a sufficient justification

of this whole discourse. 'Evangelical humility,' says Edwards in his golden *Affections*, 'is that sense which a true Christian man has of his own utter insufficiency, despicableness, and, indeed, odiousness, with an answerable frame of heart. Evangelical humiliation comes from the Spirit of God implanting and exercising supernatural and divine principles in the soul; and it comes also from a sight of the transcendent beauty of moral and spiritual things. The essence of evangelical humiliation consists in such humility as becomes a man who is in himself exceeding sinful, but who is at the same time under a dispensation of grace; it consists in a mean esteem of himself, as in himself nothing, and altogether contemptible and odious. This is the greatest and the most essential thing in personal religion. And the whole frame of the Gospel and of all God's dispensations towards fallen men are calculated, and are intended, to produce this effect in the hearts of such men.' And so on through a heart-breaking and a heart-searching chapter, such as only a master-hand could write, and such as only an evangelically-taught reader will receive and relish.

And then we have evangelical repentance, and evangelical reformation, and evangelical faith, and evangelical hope, and evangelical love, all of which are summed up in evangelical holiness.

Now, my brethren, what does all that mean to you and to me? After all that has been said— that is the question. Have we any real under-

standing of all these things? Have we any real
stake in all these things? Have we any real
delight in all these things? Are all these things
'good tidings of great joy' to us? Has God
indeed drawn you and me out of our hiding-
place of guilt and fear and shame by means of
these things? Has He come Himself to us, as
He came to Adam, and to Eve, and to Moses,
and to David? Has He evangelised us by His
grace and truth as He evangelised them? Is
Isaiah our favourite prophet? Is Paul our
favourite apostle? And are Paul's evangelical
successors our true Church Fathers? What are
our favourite psalms and hymns? Who is our
favourite preacher? And what is our favourite
doctrine? An intelligent an honest and an
evangelical answer to such questions as these
would be the very seal of the Spirit set to the
present state of our hearts before God, as also
to our prospects for eternity.

'Of all hypocrites,' says Thomas Shepard, that
pungentest of preachers, 'take good care that
you be not an evangelical hypocrite.' A hundred
times and in a hundred ways Shepard says that.
But what does the dreadful man mean? He
means this: An evangelical hypocrite is a man
who sins the more safely because grace abounds ;
who says to his lusts, both of mind and body,
that the blood of Christ cleanseth from all such
sin, and who reasons with himself thus : God
cannot, by any possibility, cast any man into hell
who loves evangelical preaching as I love it, and

who would not sit a day but in an evangelical church. My evangelical brethren, let us take good care! For if evangelical hypocrites are to be found anywhere in our day it is in a church like ours and under a doctrine like ours. At the same time, Dr. John Duncan was wont to say that he had often wished that he was as good as one of Thomas Shepard's evangelical hypocrites.

III

INTRODUCTORY : EXPERIMENTAL

EVERY schoolboy knows that Lord Bacon was the father of all our modern experimental methods in science and in philosophy. Bacon taught his students that they were no longer to seek to get at the mind of the Creator, and at the true nature of things, in any other way but by the most assiduous observation and the most unceasing experiment. Bacon was a very able man and he was a very bold man. Bacon announced to all the world that he had taken the whole domain of human knowledge for his own province ; and then to all the several branches of human knowledge he made exclusive application of his own experimental method. Bacon's supreme greatness stands in his dis- covery and in his doctrine that man is simply the student and the exponent of Nature, and that the real truth about Nature is not to be derived from any man's mere authority : no not even from the supreme authority of Aristotle himself. And thus it has come about that all the philosophies and all the sciences and all the arts of our modern world are all so observational and so experimental in their methods of study and research and operation, and consequently are all so fruitful. But all the time, our own science, my brethren, the science of personal religion, the science of the inward and the spiritual life, is by far the most important, the most universal, and the most fruitful of all the experimental sciences; and withal it is by far the oldest of all the experimental sciences, and with a record and a literature unparalleled in interest and in importance to us all.

The deeper we search into the Holy Scriptures the more experimental matter do we discover in that Divine Book. Both in the Old Testament and in the New Testament the spiritual experiences of godly men form a large part of the Sacred Record, and it gives a very fresh and a very impressive interest to many parts of the Heavenly Book when we see how much of its contents are made up of God's ways with His people as well as of their ways with Him; in other words, when we see how much of purely experimental matter is gathered up into the Word of God. In a brilliant treatise published the other year entitled *The Gospel in the Gospels*, the author applies this experimental test even to our Lord's teaching and preaching. Writing of the beatitudes in our Lord's Sermon on the Mount that fresh and penetrating writer says: ‘When our Saviour speaks to us concerning what constitutes our true blessedness He is simply de-

scribing His own experience. The beatitudes are
not the immediate revelation of His Godhead,
they are much more the impressive testimony of
His Manhood.   He knew the truth of what He
was saying, because He had verified it all in
Himself for thirty experimental years.'   Now if
that is so demonstrably true of so many of our
Lord's contributions to Holy Scripture, in the
nature of things how much more must it be true
of the experimental contributions that David and
Paul made to the same Sacred Record ? And we
ourselves are but following after them in their
great experimental methods when we give our
very closest attention to personal and spiritual
religion, both in ourselves and in all our prede-
cessors and in all our contemporaries in the life
of grace, in all lands and in all languages.

1. Now by far the deepest and by far the most
personal experience of every spiritually minded
man is his experience of his own inward sinfulness.   The sinfulness of his sin, as Paul has it ;
the malignity of his sin, the dominion that his
sin still has over him, the ungodliness and the
inhumanity of his sin, the simply indescribable
evil of his sin in every way—all that is a matter,
not of any man's doctrine and authority, all
that is the personal experience and the scientific
certainty, as we say, of every spiritually minded
man : every man, that is, who takes any true
observation of what goes on in his own heart.
The simply unspeakable sinfulness of our own
hearts is not the doctrine of David, and of

Christ, and of Paul, and of Luther, and of Calvin, and of Bunyan, and of Edwards, and of Shepard only. It is their universal doctrine—indeed it could not be otherwise—but it is also the everyday experience and the everyday agony of every man among ourselves whose eyes are at all open upon his own heart.

2. And then, if you are that spiritually enlightened man, from the day when you begin to have that heart-sore experience of yourself, you will begin to search for and to discover those great passages of Holy Scripture that contain the recorded experiences of men like yourself. 'I am dust and ashes,' said the first father of all penitent and believing and praying men. 'I am vile,' sobs Job. 'Behold, I am vile, and I will lay my hand upon my mouth. I have heard of Thee by the hearing of the ear: but now mine eye seeth Thee. Wherefore I abhor myself, and repent in dust and ashes.' And David, poor sinner, has scarcely a heart or a pen for anything else. 'There is no soundness in my flesh because of Thine anger: neither is there any rest in my bones because of my sin. My loins are filled with a loathsome disease. For, behold, I was shapen in iniquity.' And Daniel, the most blameless of men, and a man greatly beloved in heaven and on earth: 'I was left alone, and there remained no strength in me: for my comeliness was turned to corruption, and I retained no strength.' And every spiritually minded man has Paul's great experimental passage by heart: that

great experimental and autobiographic passage, which has kept so many of God's most experienced saints from absolute despair, as so many of them have testified.   Yes! there were experimental minds long before Bacon, and there was a great experimental literature long before the Essays and the Advancement and the *Instauratio Magna.*

3. And then among many other alterations of intellectual insight and spiritual taste that will come to you with your open eyes, there will be your new taste, not only for your Bible, but also for Biblical and spiritual and experimental preaching.   The spiritual preachers of our day are constantly being blamed for not tuning their pulpits to the new themes of our so progressive day.   Scientific themes are pressed upon them, and critical themes, and social themes, and such like.   But your new experience of your own sinfulness and of God's salvation ; your new need and your new taste for spiritual and experimental truth will not lead you to join in that stupid demand.   As intelligent men you will know where to find all the new themes of your new day, and you will be diligent students of them all, so far as your duty lies that way, and so far as your ability and your opportunity go ; but not on the Lord's Day and not in His house of prayer and praise.   The more inward and the more spiritual and the more experimental your own religion becomes, the more will you value inward and spiritual and experimental preaching,

and the more will you resent the intrusion into
the evangelical pulpit of those secular and passing matters that so much absorb unspiritual
men.   There is another equally impertinent
advice that our preachers are continually having
thrust upon them from the same secular and
superficial quarter, and that is that our preachers
ought entirely to drop, in our advanced and enlightened day, the old language of the Scriptures
and the creeds and the classical preachers, and
ought to substitute for it the scientific and the
journalistic jargon of the passing day. But with
your ever-deepening knowledge of yourselves,
and with the disciplined and refined taste that
will accompany such knowledge, you will rather
demand of your preachers more and more depth
of spiritual preaching and more and more purity
of spiritual style.   And then, more and more,
your estimates of preaching, and your apprecia-
tions of preachers, will have real insight and real
value and real weight with us—and will deserve
to have.

4. And then, for all doubting and sceptically
disposed persons among you, your own experience
of your own evil heart—if you will receive that
experience and will seriously attend to it—that
will prove to you the true apologetic for the
soul-saving faith of Jesus Christ. What is it
about which you are in such debate and doubt ?
Is it about the most fundamental of all facts, the
existence, and the nature, and the grace, and the
government of Almighty God ?   Well, if you are

really in earnest to know the truth, take this
way of it; this way that has brought light and
peace of mind to so many men. Turn away at
once and for ever from all your unbecoming
debates about your Maker and Preserver, and
turn to what is beyond all possible debate—your
own experience of yourselves. There is nothing
else of which you can be so sure and certain as
you are of the sin and the misery of your own
evil heart; your own evil heart so full as it is of
self-seeking, and envy, and malice, and pride,
and hatred, and revenge, and lust. And on
the other hand there is nothing of which you
can be so convinced as that love, and humility,
and meekness, and purity, and benevolence,
and brotherly kindness are your true happiness
—or would be if you could only attain to
all these beatitudes. Well, Jesus Christ came
into this world of ours at first, and He still
comes into it by His Word and by His Spirit,
in order that you may attain to all His goodness
and all His truth, and may thus escape for ever
from all your own ignorance and evil. As
William Law that prince of apologists has
it : ' Atheism is not the denial of a first Omni-
potent Cause. Real atheism is not that at all.
Real atheism is purely and solely nothing else
but the disowning, and the forsaking, and the
renouncing of the goodness, and the virtue, and
the benevolence, and the meekness of the Divine
nature : that Divine nature which has made
itself so experimental and so self-evident in

us all.   And as this experimental and self-
evident knowledge is the only sure knowledge
you can have of God, even so it is such a knowledge that it cannot be doubted or debated
away.   For it is as sure and as self-evident as
is your own experience.'   And so is it through
all the succeeding doctrines of grace and truth.
The incarnation of the Divine Son, His life, and
His death, and His resurrection, and His intercession ; and then your own life of faith and
prayer and holy obedience ; and then your
death, dear in God's sight.   Beginning with this
continually experienced need of God, all these
things will follow with an intellectual and a
moral and a spiritual demonstration that will
soon place them beyond all debate or doubt to
you.   Only know thyself, and admit the knowledge, and all else will follow as sure as the
morning sun follows the dark midnight.

5. And then in all those ways you will attain
to a religious experience of your own : a religious
experience that will be wholly and exclusively
your own.   It will not be David's experience,
nor Paul's, nor Luther's, nor Bunyan's, much as
you will study their experiences, comparing
them all with your own.   As you go deeper and
deeper into your own spiritual experience you
will gradually gather a select and an invaluable library of such experiences and you will less
and less read anything else with much interest
or gusto.   But your own unwritten experience
will all the time be your own, and in your own

spiritual experience you will have no exact fellow. For your tribulations which work in you your experiences, your tribulations are such that in all your experimental reading in the Bible or in spiritual biography or in spiritual auto-biography, you have never met the like of them. Either the writers have been afraid to speak out the whole truth about their tribulations, or, what is far more likely, they had no tribulations for a moment to match with yours. There has not been another so weak and so evil heart as yours since weak and evil hearts began to be, nor an evil life quite like yours, nor surrounding circum-stances so cross-bearing as yours, nor a sinner beset with all manner of temptations and trials behind and before like you. So much are you alone that if your fifty-first Psalm, or your seventh of the Romans, or your Confessions, or your Private Devotions, or your Grace-Abounding could ever venture to be all honestly and wholly written and published, your name would far and away eclipse them all. You do not know what a singular and what an original and what an unheard-of experience your experience is destined to be ; if only you do not break down under it, as you must not and will not do.

Begin then to make some new experiments upon a new life of faith, and of the obedience of faith ; and begin to-night. If in anything you have been following a false an unphilosophical and an unscriptural way of life, leave that wrong way at once. Be true Baconians at once—as all the true men of science will tell you to be. 'If we were religious men like you,' they will all say to you, 'we would do, and at once, what you are now being told to do. We would not debate nor doubt, but we would make experiment, and would follow out the experience.' So all the scientifically minded men will say to you. Come away then and make some new experiments from this evening. For one thing make a new experiment on secret prayer. And then come forth from your secret prayer and make immediate experiment on more love, and more patience, and more consideration for other men, and especially for the men of your own household. Make such experiments, and see if a new peace of conscience and a new happiness of heart does not begin to come to you, according to that great experimental psalm— 'Oh that my people had hearkened unto me, and Israel had walked in My ways! I should soon have subdued their enemies and turned My hand against their adversaries. He should have fed them also with the finest of the wheat: and with honey out of the rock should I have satisfied thee.'

Next Sabbath evening we shall see how Thomas Shepard made application of the experimental method both to his personal life and to his family life.

IV

'NO ONE WHO EVER CAME UNDER MY SHADOW PROSPERED'

HEN matters were not going well with Thomas Shepard in his family life he was wont to say that for his part he thought the Papists had the right way of it with their ministers. At any rate, for myself, I wish I had remained a celibate minister all my days, Shepard was wont to say to himself when anything went wrong with him in his family life. Other men, he was wont to say, might not always manage their family life very successfully, but a minister's breakdown at home was to Shepard a very tragical and a very disastrous thing. He had known many ministers, both in Old England and in New England, whose family life was a great success in every way. But that was because those ministers were such wise and good men themselves, and because they were so wise and good at managing themselves and their families. But as for himself, neither wife, nor child, nor servant, nor guest prospered, spiritually, under his shadow. So he says, again and again, in his secret journal to himself and written against himself. Nobody but himself thought that about Shepard. Many a New England minister secretly envied Shepard for his so honourable and his so happy family life. And many an unhappy wife and mother in New England dwelt in her heart on the extraordinary happiness of Thomas Shepard's manse. All the same, never was there more sincerity or more poignancy in any heartbroken confession than when Shepard entered it again and again in his most private papers—that under the blighting shadow of his presence neither old nor young ever really prospered. Thales was so fond of children that nothing would persuade him to become a father. And though Thomas Shepard became the father of more children than one, he loved and pitied his children so much that he often wished they had never been born: at any rate to him.

1. As I go over and over Thomas Shepard's Meditations and Spiritual Experiences I find these four faults of his filling Shepard's heart and conscience with a great remorse. First, his too great love for his books and his too much time spent in his study. Had Shepard been a celibate priest instead of a Protestant and Puritan pastor, his love for his books and his long hours in his study would all have been to be commended. But with his family neglected, his pulpit and his class studies became his besetting sin. He laments in one place his 'ragged style' in writing, as well he may. But far better

write a ragged style than bring up and send out
ragged children into the world. Shepard lived
among his books before he was married, and he
continued to live too much among them after
he was a married man and a father of a family.
And that bad habit of his was very near being
the ruin of his household life. Ministers, says
Samuel Rutherford, of all men are made up of
extremes. Some ministers ruin themselves and
their families and their people, and all beyond
redemption, by their sinful neglect of their sacred
studies. And then there is one minister here
and another there like Thomas Shepard, who
imperil their own and their children's souls by
their intemperate and untimeous devotion to
their books and to their desks. But the beauty
of Thomas Shepard was that he discovered his
mistake and set himself to rectify his mistake
before it was too late. He continued to love his
books and to labour at his sermons, but he gave
more and more time and thought to make his
children living epistles to be known and read of
all men. You are not ministers and you do not
have the peculiar temptations of ministers. But
you are bankers, and lawyers, and merchants,
and schoolmasters and so on ; and, withal, many
of you are great lovers of good books. Now
Thomas Shepard, though he has been over two
centuries dead, comes back to-night to warn you
that no bank, and no office, and no shop, and no
book, must steal away your time and your thought
and your affection from your wife and your

children. And if that has been your temptation in the past, take this of the remorseful Psalmist for your prayer and for your vow henceforth : ' O when wilt thou come to me ? And I will behave myself in a perfect way. I will walk within my house with a perfect heart.'

2. Shepard was not an ordinary man in anything, and least of all in his family worship. Now though you would not expect it of such a man his family worship caused Shepard many a remorseful moment. Never was that Prophetic and Puritan ordinance observed better than by the New England fathers, and every one would have said never better than in Thomas Shepard's New England manse. But he did not think so himself. Like all thinking men who take that first of family duties aright to heart, as his family grew up, Shepard keenly felt the ever-increasing difficulty of performing that family duty as it ought to be performed. That is to say, he felt the ever-increasing difficulty of his being able to interest, and to instruct, and to impress, and to carry along with him all his household, rightly dividing the word of truth to each several one of them, from the youngest to the oldest, and from the stable-boy to the student. We know how well Thomas Halyburton succeeded in family worship in spite of all his difficulties. ' Most willingly I engaged in that duty, and when I was engaged in it my soul often made me like the chariots of Amminadib. I was not easily stopped. I failed sometimes in the

just bounds. But with all my mistakes, as far
as I reckon, it was about this time that the Lord
first began to commend Himself and His worship
to Lady Anne Elcho, which made her at her
death to bless the Lord for my family worship.'
And Shepard's three sons all blessed the Lord
at their death for their father's family worship
also, though their irregularity at it, and their
irreverence during it, had often given their father
a sore heart. But he never blamed any of them
for that so much as he blamed himself. No! he
often said to himself as he went back to his
books after another unsuccessful effort at family
worship: No! no one prospers, either in family
worship or in anything else, under my all-
blighting shadow!

3. Another thing that filled poor Shepard's
heart and conscience with an ever-running sore
was his life-long failure to speak in time and to
speak aright to his children about their own
personal religion. He often tried to come round
upon that matter in his family readings of the
Word, and in his family prayers, but wholly
without result. Not one of his children seemed
to him to be one atom the better of all his
expositions and all his exhortations and all his
prayers. His servants often acknowledged what
they owed to the family worship of the New
Cambridge manse, and his guests would often
write back to tell him the same thing, but never
wife nor child to the day of his death. Was it
any wonder that he wrote that terrible sentence

about his baleful shadow again and again and with secret tears! Because, as I have told you, in all this he blamed nobody but himself. 'I wanted wisdom to speak to them aright, and I put it off till it was too late. I could not find the right time in which to do it, nor the right way in which to do it, till time went on and it was not done at all.' At their latest and best I do not find in Shepard's extant Experiences anything so happy as was the experience of a minister friend of mine in the Highlands to whom his son explained and said: 'It was your own family worship, father, that did it to me!' 'I saw,' wrote Shepard, 'what a blessing it would be if my son's salvation came to him through me.' And his eldest son's salvation did at last come to him. And I shall continue to believe that it came to him, somehow, through his father, though the family papers that are extant do not say whether it was through his father's so-awakening pulpit work or through his so well-studied family worship, or most likely through his father's so heart-chastened walk and conversation both at home and abroad. Enough that his salvation came in time, both to Shepard's eldest son and to his two brothers. Before they were born Shepard had set his whole heart on having all his three sons to be New England ministers. And after many appearances the other way he at last got his whole heart's desire. And that because, as he so boldly said, he would not let God off from one of His promises concerning

his sons. 'I will not let Thee go in this matter
of my sons!' so Shepard would sometimes wrestle
about this one thing till the daybreak. There
had been a long time during which there was not
the slightest prospect of his importunate and
concentrated prayer ever being answered. But
though he does not himself say so in any of his
papers that I have found, I have reason to believe
that it was on the very night on which he first
wrote this about his all-blighting shadow, and
that with an ink of sweat and tears, that the
tide began to turn in respect of his three sons.
As he saw his three sons setting out, one after
another, to the Harvard Hall, I hear their en-
raptured father taking back all his hard speeches
about God, and indeed all his hard speeches
about himself and his sons, and substituting in
place of those hard speeches such a psalm as this:
'Gracious is the Lord and righteous: Yea, our
God is merciful. The Lord preserveth the
simple: I was brought low, and He helped me.
O Israel, thou hast destroyed thyself, but in Me
is thy help.'

4. Yet another thing that caused Shepard
great sadness of heart was his constitutional
gloom of mind and his too melancholy tempera-
ment taken along with his so easily crossed
temper. Altogether, substitute Thomas Shepard
the New England Puritan, for Santa Teresa the
Spanish Superior, and you will have his exact
case, as he saw and felt it to be, in his home life.
Thomas Shepard could not express himself so well

as Santa Teresa could, but in substance and essence they both say the same thing. ' My children,' she said on her death-bed, ' you must pardon me much. You must pardon me most of all the bad example I have given you. Do not imitate me. Do not live as I have lived. I have been the greatest sinner in all Spain. I have not kept the laws that I have made for other people. I beseech you, my daughters, for the love of God, that you keep the rules of your holy house as I have never kept them. But, then, the sacrifices of God are a broken spirit: a broken and a contrite heart Thou, O God, wilt not despise.' Thomas Shepard and Teresa of Jesus would not have spoken to one another on earth. But they are now praising God together in glory, and are continually saying : ' By Thy great grace to us here are we ourselves, and all the spiritual children that Thou didst give us.'

V

'THE MORE I DO THE WORSE I AM'

WHEN Dr. Chalmers was at Skirling on one occasion he went to the village school and gave the children an elementary lesson in optical science. Taking the black-board and a piece of chalk he drew a long diameter on the board and then he ran a large circumference around the diameter. And then in his own imaginative and dramatic way turning to the children he said to them, 'You must all see that the longer the diameter of light the larger is the surrounding circumference of darkness. And in like manner the shorter the diameter of light the smaller is the circumference of the surrounding darkness.' Now all we have to do this evening is to carry over that striking illustration from the region of mathematical and optical things to the region of moral and spiritual things and we shall have Thomas Shepard's religious experience set before us in a way we shall never forget. The more that Shepard does, that is to say, the longer his diameter of duty done the larger is the circumference of duty he has still to do. And the holier his heart becomes the more sinful the remaining corruption of his heart becomes to him, till he cries out like the holiest of men, O wretched man that I am!

Our best way will be to go to Thomas Shepard himself for an outstanding instance of this painful experience of his and this remorseful admission of his. And perhaps the best instance of all his instances is his lifelong experience of the exceeding sinfulness of his Sabbath days. Never did the most conscientious preacher do more than Shepard did to prepare himself every new week for a fruitful and a happy Sabbath, both to his people and to himself. Shepard was a hard worker both in his pastoral visitations and in his study. He took the very greatest pains in the preparation of his sermons. He had an intellectual and a spiritual people, he respected and revered his people, and he worked hard for them. It was his rule to work hard early in the week and as a rule he had his sermons ready by two o'clock on Saturday afternoon. And then he gave up the whole of the Saturday evening and Sabbath morning to prepare his own mind and heart for his pulpit duties on the coming day. These are Shepard's own severe words on this subject: 'God will surely curse that minister who lumbers up and down the world all the week and then thinks to prepare for his pulpit by a hurried hour or two on Saturday night and Sabbath morning. Whereas, God knows, Saturday night and Sabbath morning were little enough time in which to weep

and to pray and to get his sinful soul into a fit
frame for the approaching day.' And when some
young ministers came to see Shepard on his
deathbed he said to them: 'Your work, remember, is a great work ; and it demands great
seriousness of mind on your part. For my own
part,' he went on, 'I always sought to get good
to my own soul in composing my sermons. And
I always went to the pulpit as if it were my last
sermon before I went to give an account of my
ministry to God.' Now after all that, you would
have felt sure that Shepard would always have
had the best ministerial conscience in all New
England, and the happiest and the sweetest of
Sabbath days and Sabbath nights. But as a
matter of fact it was the very opposite of that.
In all autobiography I have never come across
such sad reading as are Shepard's Sabbath night
entries in his secret journal. Entry after entry
is made with the sweat of an agonised conscience
and with the blood of a broken heart, till I shall
not attempt to tell you his terrible self-accusa-
tions all the Sabbath day and all the Sabbath
night. How his first and last thought all Sabbath
was *himself*, and not God nor God's people. How
he was puffed up, like a born fool, if he thought
he had got on well in his prayers and in his
sermons, and then how he was like Heman himself
in his misery if he had not had enough eloquence
and impressiveness that day in his pulpit. How
he fished for his people's praise after a successful
sermon, and how his heart was like dust and

ashes all night if no one had flattered him.
' Vile ! vile ! vile !' he cries a thousand times in
his Sabbath night papers.   His abominable self-
seeking, his miserable thought of his own glory
in all he did, made Shepard gnash his teeth at
himself as if he were in hell.   In his own words,
he was ' in the deepest hell ' on many a Sabbath
night. Samuel Rutherford, like Thomas Shepard,
was a born preacher.   But his indwelling sin, in
his case also, poisoned all his Sabbaths and made
his Anwoth pulpit the greatest temptation of
his much-tempted life. There is a proverb to the
effect that, when the best things become corrupt,
there you have corruption indeed.   And so both
Shepard and Rutherford experienced it to be in
the matter of their pulpit work.   Do what they
would they could not keep the thought of *themselves* out of their minds even in their most
sanctified services.   And that corrupted and
polluted the pulpit to those two saints of God
in a way and to a degree that only a saintly and
at the same time a self-seeking preacher will
ever understand and believe. Rutherford often
wondered, in his own passionate way, that he had
not been eaten up of worms in his pulpit, as
Herod was on his throne, and for the very same
reason. The more that Shepard and Rutherford
did to prepare for their preaching, and the more
they sought God's glory while they were engaged
in their preaching, the more they felt themselves
to be the vilest of all men. And there was a
third minister in that day of that same mind

about himself. 'One of my best friends,' writes
Shepard, 'and one of the best men now living on
the earth, has said to me that if the Lord, out of
His grace, does not save him, he is undone for
ever. For his heart and his whole nature are
against God; and the more he does of God's
command and will, the worse he discovers his
heart and whole nature within him to be.' Those
were three very wretched ministers : four, count-
ing the Apostle Paul. For, as Dr. Chalmers
would have said, the longer their diameter of
preparation and prayer for their pulpits the more
did those four devoted ministers cry out every
Sabbath day, Who is sufficient for these things!
And the more their innermost hearts were cleansed
clear of themselves and their self-seeking, the
more did every remaining drop of themselves
make them to lie on their faces before God all
Sabbath night sobbing and saying : O wretched
men that we are! Who shall deliver us from
this body of death ? Many more instances of
this same thing crowd in upon me till I have no
room for them. Take this one more instance,
and this time out of our own Thomas Boston.
' My Sabbath day duties were enough of themselves to damn me : my Sabbath day duties
must all be washed along with myself in the sin-
atoning Blood. The first impression on my
spirit after I came down from the pulpit was
my utter inability to escape from my sinfulness
of heart. I saw that it was as possible for a rock
to lift itself up to heaven as it was for me to

raise my heart to true holiness.' So says the truly
holy Thomas Boston about himself; 'that truly
great Scottish divine,' says Jonathan Edwards.

But my brethren, all this time an ounce of
your own experience is better than a ton of testimony from other men. Now among so many
now present there must surely be some of you
who know in yourselves the terrible truth of
what Shepard says. There was a time, was there
not? when you did not feel any sin, or any guilt,
or any shame, or any remorse, whatever you said
or did. As Paul has it in his great journal of
his own experience, the law of true spiritual
holiness had not yet entered your evil heart.
But ever since that holy law has entered your
evil heart, as the Apostle says about himself,
you, like him, have died. That is to say, the
more you now do to fulfil that law of true holiness the more you have to do that you can never
hope to do. Nowadays, as spiritually-minded
Thomas Boston has it, the best thing you ever
do would be enough to damn you, were judgment
laid to the line and righteousness to the plummet.
There is so much of *yourself* in the best things
you do and so little of God and His glory.
Jonathan Edwards, Thomas Shepard's spiritual
scholar, has drawn your spiritual portrait to
perfection as you now are. 'The more,' says
Edwards, 'a true saint loves God with a truly
gracious love, the more he desires to love Him,
and the more miserable he is at his want of love
to Him. The more he hates sin, the more he

desires to hate it. The more he mourns for sin, the more he longs to mourn for it. The more his heart is broken for sin, the more he prays that it may be far more broken. The more he hungers and thirsts after God, the more he faints and fails in seeking after God. Forgetting those things that are behind, he ever reaches forth to those things that are still before. He ever presses toward the far-off mark.' To take a familiar instance out of your own experience. You will take up your secret cross for weeks and months and that without a frown or a murmur or even a sigh that any mortal ear hears. But after a long season of the sweetest submission and the most spontaneous and spiritual obedience some day, and most unaccountably to you, something happens to you and to your cross, and, in a moment, a great outbreak of rebellion and bitterness fills your heart. All you have suffered in the past, all you have attained to of submission and resignation in the past, seems to you to have been lost in a moment. So it often seemed to Paul also, and to Shepard, and to Rutherford, and to Boston, and to Chalmers. But it is not so. The truth is, it is because you have borne your cross so bravely, and have suffered under it so nobly, that the remaining dregs of your rebellion are so bitter to your sanctified heart. It is because the blessed law of resignation and submission has gone so deep into your renewed heart that the spots of sin still remaining there are so black and so bitter to you to bear. The diameter

of your holy obedience has been so long and so
beautiful that the darkness that still hangs
around it is so dark and dense to you.

Or again, is your besetting sinfulness not so
much your rebellion at your daily cross, as, say,
Asaph's besetting sin of envying and grieving at
the prosperity of some neighbouring man? Or
is it a heart as dark as hell with ill-will at some
neighbouring man? Or is it a revengeful and an
unforgiving heart at some such man? Then here
also the Apostle's great principle comes in, the
law enters and consequently the sinfulness of
your heart abounds. And here also Dr. Chalmers'
blackboard illustration comes in, and in this way.
The more honest delight you try to have in
another man's prosperity, and the less and less
ill-will you try to feel toward your enemy, and
the more you are able to forgive your enemy
even to seventy times seven, the more you are
tortured with the secret remainders of envy and
malice and revenge in your heart; the longer the
diameter of love the larger the circumference of
the evil feeling still remaining in your unsanctified heart. You are under that most blessed law
which so orders the spiritual life that as long as
any dregs of secret sinfulness still dwell in your
heart you feel as if there was nothing but a
hopeless sinfulness in your heart. Like Bishop
Andrewes, you feel as if you were actually 'made
of sin,' and as if not one atom of true holiness
had ever entered into your composition at all.
That is your deepest feeling about yourself;

whereas the real truth is no man will ever taste what true holiness of heart is but by passing through the same experience of sin as your experience, which was the experience of Paul also, and Shepard, and Rutherford, and Boston, and Chalmers. In the experience of all such men the holy law of God enters deeper and deeper and deeper every day, till the remaining sinfulness of their heart abounds every day. But then when such remaining sinfulness abounds, grace much more abounds, that as your sinfulness hath reigned unto your death, even so might grace reign through righteousness unto your eternal life by Jesus Christ your Lord.

'Truly to see and to feel indwelling sin is the torture of all tortures,' said Luther, who knew that torture by a lifelong experience of it. And yet neither Luther nor any other spiritually-minded man would for one moment exchange that fearful torture, no not for a bed of roses. The truly spiritual man lies down on his lifelong rack, and actually loves it, because he believes that to him perfect and everlasting holiness of heart lies beyond it. Bear up, then, O sin-tortured soul! For it is but for a moment. Bear up, because it will assuredly work in you and for you an exceeding and an eternal weight of glory. Your never-to-be-told sufferings because of your remaining sinfulness are a sure token to you that you are far on in the way that leadeth, and that alone leadeth, to everlasting life. Keep up your heart then amid all your agony of heart, for eye hath not seen nor ear heard what God hath prepared for sufferers like you. Life-long agony and all, you have not received the spirit of bondage again to fear, but you have received the Spirit of adoption. The Spirit also bearing witness with your spirit that you are the children of God. And if children, then heirs: heirs of God, and joint-heirs with Christ: if so be that you suffer with Him, that you may be also glorified together.

I ask'd the Lord that I might grow
   In faith, and love, and every grace:
Might more of His salvation know,
   And seek more earnestly His face.

I hoped that in some favour'd hour
   At once He'd answer my request,
And, by His love's constraining power,
   Subdue my sins and give me rest.

Instead of that, He made me feel
   The hidden evils of my heart,
And let the angry powers of hell
   Assault my soul in every part.

'Lord, why is this?' I trembling cried,
   'Wilt thou pursue a worm to death?'
'Tis in this way,' the Lord replied,
   'I answer prayer for grace and faith.

These inward trials I employ
   From self and sin to set thee free:
To break thy scheme of earthly joy
   That thou mayst seek thy all in Me.'

VI

'IT IS SOMETIMES SO WITH ME THAT I WILL RATHER DIE THAN PRAY'

SUPPOSE for a moment that we had been left without hope in our fallen estate of sin and misery. Just suppose that we had been left as a race with nothing before us but a fearful looking for of judgment. And then suppose we were told that there was another race of sinful and miserable men exactly like ourselves in one of those wonderful worlds that we see in our midnight sky. And suppose we were told also that to them in their fallen state their Maker had Himself become their Redeemer and had prepared His throne in the heavens, so that by simply approaching that throne they could command His ear and His heart and His hand at any hour of the day and in any watch of the night. Suppose all that had been told us about those happy creatures, with what holy wonder and with what holy desire would we have gone out of our house at night and looked up at that far-off star! How would we have envied those

highly favoured sons of God! O that my lot
had been cast among them, and not on this God-
forsaken earth! What Sabbath days they must
have up there! What communion seasons!
What meetings for prayer and praise! And
what family worship! How happy it must be
to be a father up there! How sweet and blessed,
above all words, to be a mother! But suppose
we were also assured that with all that, those so
privileged people simply despised and neglected
their Maker and Redeemer and absolutely hated
so much as to kneel down before Him. Suppose
we were assured that ninety-nine out of every
hundred of those redeemed men actually rose
every morning and lay down every night as if
there were no God and no mercy-seat—what
would you have said about such men? You
would have said that they must be madmen, if
the tenth part of what you have been told about
them is true.

Now, not only is it all true, but more than
that, this world of ours is that wonderful star.
And we who are assembled in this House of God
this Sabbath evening, we are those suicides. It
is we who say, What is the Almighty that we
should serve Him? And what profit should we
have if we prayed to Him? Now, if all that is
so, can any explanation be given of that so fearful
state of matters?—a state of matters so fearful
that one of the most prayerful men that ever
lived here confesses to us that it is sometimes
so with him that he will rather face death and

judgment than abide for long before God in
secret prayer. Now can that awful state of
matters be at all explained? And if so what
can that explanation by any possibility be?

Well, at bottom and to begin with, there is
some absolutely unaccountable alienation of our
sinful hearts away from our Maker and our
Redeemer. There is some utterly inexplicable
estrangement from God that has, somehow, taken
possession of your heart and mine. There is
some dark mystery of iniquity here that has
never yet been sufficiently cleared up. There is
some awful 'enmity against God,' as the Holy
Ghost has it: some awful malice that sometimes
makes us hate the very thought of God. We
hate God, indeed, much more than we love ourselves. For we knowingly endanger our immortal
souls; every day and every night we risk death
and hell itself rather than come close to God
and abide in secret prayer. This is the spiritual
suicide that we could not have believed possible
had we not discovered it in our own atheistical
hearts. The thing is far too fearful to put into
words. But put into words for once, this is what
our everyday actions say concerning us in this
supreme matter of prayer. 'No; not to-night,'
we say, 'I do not need to pray to-night. I am
really very well to-night. My heart is much
steadier in its beats to-night. And besides I
have business on my hands that will take up all
my time to-night. I have quite a pile of unanswered letters on my table to-night. And

before I sleep I have the novel of the season to finish, for I must send it back to-morrow morning. And besides there is no such hurry as all that. I am not so old nor so frail as all that. Go thy way for this time, when I have a convenient season I will call for thee.'

But even when it is not so bad with us as that, at our very best there is a certain backwardness in prayer to which all praying men have to confess. I find that same sad confession in men so different both in their doctrines and in their experiences as Jeremy Taylor and John Newton. These are the very words of the eloquent Bishop in his *Holy Living*: 'There is no worse sign of our spiritual danger than the backwardness we have to pray. So weary are we of the duty, so glad are we to have it over, and so witty are we to find an excuse to evade it.' And these are the exact words of John Newton in his fine book, *The Cardiphonia*: 'I find in my own case an unaccountable backwardness to pray. I can read, I can write, I can converse with a ready will, but secret prayer is far more spiritual than any of these. And the more spiritual any duty is the more my carnal heart is apt to start away from it.' Both of those prayerful men, you see, confess to a sad backwardness in prayer—to call that state of mind and heart by no worse name.

Now in a state of matters like that it is quite evident how next to impossible it will be for any man to put his whole heart into his prayer, even when he compels himself to pray. And yet

without the whole heart it is not true prayer at
all. It is only when we seek God with our whole
heart, that we have any assurance from Him that
we shall find Him. The men of Judah, we read,
swore to God with their whole heart. They
sought God with their whole heart's desire and
He was found of them and He gave them rest
round about. And a psalmist sings of the great
blessedness of them that keep God's testimonies,
and that seek Him with their whole heart. And
again, With my whole heart have I sought Thee,
O let me not wander from Thy commandments.
And again, When you seek Me with your whole
heart, then shall you find Me. Even the old
Stoics, who lived in an outside dispensation, said
that nothing cost them so much as the things
which they purchased by prayer. Because they
had to give up their whole heart to their prayer
before they could gain anything from God in
that way. And our own New England Shepard
has this same experience in the New Testament
dispensation. 'August 13. I saw that my heart
was prone to neglect prayer. I soon thought
that I had prayed enough for one night. Till
I came to see that all I could pray was little
enough to help down all the mercy I needed.
And till I came to see also that God would have
me to get my mercy from Him at some cost to
myself.' Yes; this is one of the great difficulties
of a life of prayer to such men as we are, that it
demands from us our whole heart.

Then again, sometimes, and to some people,

there is the great difficulty they have in praying along with some other people. For instance, you will have an insurmountable difficulty sometimes in entering with your whole heart into public worship. Your minister does not carry you with him in his pulpit devotions. His language, his voice, his accent, his intonation, his manner, his composition, or some other unacceptableness of his to you, throws you wholly out of step with him till you lose all the help of public prayer. Then again, those who conduct family prayers at home do not help you, rather otherwise. They are so familiar to you, they so little interest you, they are so lengthy, and they so weary you, and so on. Till family worship is no worship at all to you, but the very opposite, and till you escape away from it as often as you can. Then again, and still more distressful, when a husband and his wife attempt to pray together, or a father and his son, or a mother and her daughter, their personal needs at the moment, their personal experiences at the moment are so unlike, their innermost lives are so different and so unshared, that it is impossible for them to agree together in what they ask and in the way they ask for it. Till all their attempts at united prayer only bring out the more painfully how far away they are from one another, and thus from God. So many, so real, and sometimes so absolutely un- avoidable are the difficulties that lie in the way of a life of true and prevailing prayer.

And once more, why do the most devout of

men and the most long-exercised of men sometimes so fall away from their life of prayer and
from all liberty and comfort and power in prayer,
and that after they have for years so enjoyed all
that ? Well, that is a question in personal and
experimental religion that I cannot answer satis-
factorily to myself, as yet. I have tried hard to
find out some of the reasons for that declension,
both in myself and in other men, but I am not
satisfied with what I have found, as yet. If I
succeed in my study of that painful matter, I
shall tell you more about it another time.

From all that let us proceed to ask how that
awful state of matters is to be met and overcome
by us. For it would be too terrible to think
that our dislike of prayer and our neglect of
God is to go on till death and till we are suddenly
summoned to give an account of our life of
prayer, as of all else.

1. Well, for one thing—'I thought on my
ways,' says the devout and much experienced
psalmist, ' and I turned my feet into Thy testimonies.' Let us be like him in this matter of
prayer. Let us think on our ways in prayer.
Let us think on the place that prayer holds in
Holy Scripture, and on the place that prayer
has always held in the lives of all God's outstanding people. Let us think of the urgency
and the grace of God's commands laid on us to
live a life of prayer. Let us think that the
Almighty is actually waiting for us to begin to
pray in order that He may begin to be gracious

to us in answer to our prayers. Let us think how
we must look in His eyes in this matter of
prayer. Let us think what He must think and
say to Himself about us. Let us think if we
were in His place what we would think of any
one who treated us and our son as we treat Him
and His Son. We could not fail to cry to God
for the spirit of grace and of supplication if we
would only begin to think Who and What He
is, and who and what we are, and what prayer is
appointed by Him to be between Him and us.

2. And then, when once you begin to think
and to pray, be sure you persevere in it to the
end. Never never in this world give up prayer.
And the more distaste and difficulty you find in
beginning to pray the more liberty and sweetness you will taste if you only persevere. ' Men
plead difficulty,' says Shepard, ' I plead advantage. For he that overcometh his indisposition
to pray shall eat of the hidden manna. Have
you not yourselves,' he asks us, ' eaten of this
same hidden manna. Have there not been times
when you were very unwilling to begin to pray,
but after you began and persevered but a little
you could not leave off ? ' Yes ; that is the recorded experience of one who sometimes would
rather risk dying in his sin than begin to pray.
What Pascal said of composition is still more
true of prayer, the difficulty is to make a good
beginning.

3. Then again, go on in your prayer in spite
of your want of present gusto, so Santa Teresa

is continually counselling her spiritual children. Samuel Rutherford shall explain to us what the Spanish saint means by gusto in prayer. When the devout parishioners of Kilmacolm complained to Rutherford concerning their too little sweetness in prayer this was the counsel he returned to his correspondents. 'The less sweetness in prayer the more pure spirituality. A sweet service has not seldom its sweetness and gusto from some other source than the spiritual world? I believe,' wrote Rutherford, 'that many think that prayer is formal and lifeless unless the wind is in the west, and unless all their sails are filled with spiritual joy. But I am not of their mind who so think,' said that great counsellor of Scottish souls in their distresses and in their apprehensions.

4. 'July 2,' writes Shepard, 'I saw it to be my duty not only to pray from time to time, but actually to *live by prayer*. To live by prayer for myself, and for my family, and for my church. And I saw that my heart was at last conformed to the mind and the will of God in that respect. And I went on to consider in what ways I might henceforth live by prayer alone.' 'Pray often,' says Taylor, 'and you will pray oftener, till you will end in praying without ceasing.'

5. Again, always make hay when the sun shines. As thus: And the LORD descended and proclaimed the name of the LORD. And when Moses heard the name of the LORD, he made haste, and bowed his head to the earth, and wor-

shipped God, and said, If now I have found grace in thy sight, pardon our sin and our iniquity, and take us for Thine inheritance.   Yes; make haste to make hay when the sun shines.

6. Again if you are an experienced man in these spiritual matters you will be able to turn both your past transgressions and your present temptations to your greater prosperity in the life of prayer. ' My sin is ever before me,' said David, when he was engaged on the composition of his greatest psalm. ' I am always sinning,' said Luther, ' and I am always reading the Epistle to the Romans, and am always praying.'

7. And again, when you ask the advice of the old experts in this matter they will all tell you to set apart a special time for prayer, and even a special place. James Durham, the laird of Pourie Castle, gave himself much to spiritual reading. And he caused build a study for himself on the head of the stair in his house in the country, three miles out the Forfar road on the way out of Dundee. In this little chamber that great scholar, great divine, and great saint gave himself continually to reading and meditation and prayer, and he was so close a student that he often forgot to eat his bread even after his servant had set it on his table. And like Durham the New England Fathers were wont to build their houses with a secret room for secret prayer. And Shepard looked on it as a sure sign of declension when the New England architects got no orders to put such secret rooms in their plans for new houses.

8. Speaking about secret rooms and secret
prayers, a friend of mine has this devotional
device put up on his most shut-in wall. He has
a long picture-frame with the portraits of all his
family fixed into the frame from the oldest to
the youngest. And then hanging above that
frame he has a fine head of Jesus Christ, which is
so hung that the Intercessor looks down night
and day on the children's portraits below as if
He were making continual intercession for them,
as indeed He is. And instead of that standing
in room of his own secret prayer for his children
and thus discharging him from it as we might
think the danger was, my friend assures me that
the sight of that wall night and morning draws
him down to his knees, when but for that re-
minding and quickening wall he would often
forget to pray. You might try some such device
yourselves, as many of you as have a bad conscience both toward God and toward your
children in this matter of secret and intercessory
prayer in their behalf.

What are these, and whence came they? These
are they who were born and brought up in a
baptized home, but were never prayed for, to call
prayer, and were never taught to pray for themselves. They took a high place at school and at
college but they were never taught to pray.
Their fathers and their mothers were church
members, but they never took the trouble to
teach their children to pray. And when they

became fathers and mothers themselves the entail of prayerlessness and neglect of God descended to their children also. Therefore they are where they are. And therefore it is with them and with their children as it is. My brethren, if prayer is anything at all it is everything. And that is exactly what the whole Word of God says about prayer; it is everything, absolutely everything.

VII

'MY OWN IDLE WORDS IN MY PREACH- ING, IN MY PRAISE, AND IN MY PRAYER, AND THE ACCOUNT I GIVE OF THEM TO GOD'

WORDS, to begin with, are very wonderful things. Among all our wonderful things there is nothing more wonderful than our words. For all we think within ourselves we think by means of words. And when we tell out our thoughts to other men we do so by means of words. All we read and all we hear and all we pray and all we praise we do it all by means of words. Without words indeed we the children of men and the sons of God would be as the beasts that perish. And much more wonderful than all that, when the Holy Ghost takes most profoundly of the things of Christ and reveals them to us, of all the great names and noble titles He gives to the Son of God He gives Him no name and no title that is so full of all magnificence and all nobleness and all wonder- fulness as when He names Him The Word—The

E

Word of God.   In the beginning was the Word,
and the Word was with God, and the Word
was God.

> Amid the eternal silences
>   God's endless Word was spoken ;
> None heard but He who always spake,
>   And the silence was unbroken.
>
> O marvellous !   O worshipful !
>   No song nor sound is heard,
>   But everywhere, and every hour,
>   In love, in wisdom, and in power,
> The Father speaks His dear Eternal Word.

But of all the multitudinous kinds and varieties
and qualities of our words our Lord in one of His
sermons singles out and denounces what He char-
acterises as 'idle words.'   Now what exactly does
our Lord mean by idle words ?   There can be no
mystery about that.   For idle words are just idle
words.   Idle words are just those words of ours
that do no work.   They stand all the day idle.
They perform no appointed task.   They bring no
help to men and they contribute no glory to God.
But our Lord specially brands and denounces all
those words of ours that are so idle and so worthless and so hypocritical and so offensive in our
pretended worship of God.   All our idle words of
all kinds will have to be given an account of one
day, but above all those divine words and those
human words about divine persons and divine
things that we so idly take up on our idle lips.
It is of the greatest and the best words in heaven

and on earth that our Lord speaks in such
scathing language, when He says that of every
such word we speak so idly and so irreverently
we shall be called upon to give an account thereof
in the day of judgment.

But before we enter on any of our greatest and
best words, let us begin with our very worst
word, that worst word in our whole world of
words, our own worst word Sin. Let us begin
with that worst of words because it is the true and
it is the only keyword, it is the true and it is the
only password into every other word, good and
bad, human and divine. For just as our bodily
diseases alone explain and alone justify and alone
account for all our physicians with all their vocabu-
laries of diseases as well as all their medical training,
and all their instruments of healing and all their
operations and all their medicines and all their
treatments of their patients, just so Sin, our
spiritual disease, alone explains and justifies and
fully accounts for our Divine Physician with all
His authoritative and true vocabulary and all
His instruments and all His medicines; all His
sin-atoning blood, and all His regenerating and
sanctifying Spirit, with all His other divine and
soul-saving means of grace and truth. And thus
it is that God always begins with our sin when
He would truly save us. And thus it is that till
we see sin somewhat aright, and think about sin
somewhat aright, and speak about sin somewhat
aright, all our other words in that whole world of
things, and indeed in every other world of things

will be idle and worse than idle in the sight of God and in the last judgment of Jesus Christ. Now with all that the simple and incontestable truth is that among all our idle words there is no word so idle in most men's mouths as just this most awful of all words, Sin. 'All men see and speak the word Sin,' says Shepard, that past master of the subject, 'but few men see the thing.' No man indeed has ever seen Sin aright; no man but that one Man who was made Sin. But at the same time to those men who have seen even a little into the exceeding sinfulness of sin, to them from that time all other words in the moral and spiritual worlds, and indeed in all other worlds, henceforth take on a new reality, a new sincerity, a new height and a new depth. 'Paul,' says Shepard, 'was a Pharisee till he saw sin.' But when once he saw sin and his own sinfulness, from that time he became the Paul that all true and great sinners know so well and love so much. And thus it is that all Paul's apostolical successors in the pulpit labour to bring home to all men that new sight and sense that makes a new man, the sight and sense of sin. For just in the measure and just in the intensity that any man sees sin, and his own sinfulness in its guilt and in its malignity and in its deadliness, just in that measure and just in that inwardness and just in that intensity will all he reads and all he hears about God's salvation become every day the best of news to him. But on the other hand take any evangelical and experimental scripture you like, take any prayer or psalm or hymn you like, and they will all be so many absolutely idle words to you unless you first see and feel yourself to be a sinner and the chief of sinners. Go over all God's words of salvation and you will see that to be so. Go back to the beginning and take the pascal lamb and its sprinkled blood, take the brazen serpent and its healing power, take the sin-broken psalmist and his Fifty-first Psalm, take the evangelical prophet and his Fifty-third chapter, take John the Baptist and his 'Behold the Lamb of God,' take the Lamb of God Himself, from His cradle to His cross, and from His cross to His throne; take Paul and his great Epistles, take Luther and his Pauline doctrines, and so on all through our truest theology, our truest preaching, and our truest religious literature; and all that glorious world of things, with all its glorious words, all is full of idleness to him who has not the true key to all these things in his own awful and unspeakable sinfulness. But that happiest of men who has that true and only key of all these things in himself, and who takes that key and puts it out to constant use, he will thereby be able to unlock, both for himself and for other men, all the treasures of grace and truth that are laid up in Jesus Christ. 'The distinction,' says an able Anglican divine, 'which our Lord and the New Testament continually make, is not that some men are sinners and some are not. But that some men are so content to be sinners that they do not know they are sinners. While some other men are so convicted and convinced of their own sinfulness that they are conscious of nothing else in themselves but their sin. Blessed are we,' he continues, 'even that we are sinners, if we see and know our sin; if through knowledge of the curse of sin we have been brought to know the supreme blessedness of holiness. For beings like ourselves the consummate joy of holiness would be incomprehensible and impossible, save through a corresponding and an equal sense of sin. All our true joy,' he adds, 'in what we are yet to be is born of our true sorrow for what we now are.'

There is a well-known aphorism in our English literature which, if we would only carry it over into our religious literature and would continually practice it would change everything; that would in course of time transform all our religious words from all their present idleness to a great fruitfulness and a great acceptableness. 'Read,' so the fine aphorism runs, 'Read always with your eye on the object.' That is to say, read not so much with your eye on the words as on the things. And the best literary critic of the past generation has said in illustration of that aphorism that Homer, his blindness and all, stands at the head of all subsequent poets simply because he always sang with his whole inward eye fastened on the thing about which he was singing. But we do not need to go so far afield as Homer. For we have another man of that same genius, John Bunyan. Hear him: 'There was not one part of the Gospel of the Lord Jesus but I was orderly led into it. For always as I read it methought I was as if I had *seen* Him born; as if I had *seen* Him grow up; as if I had *seen* Him walk through this world from His cradle to His cross; to which also, when He came, I *saw* how gently He gave Himself to be nailed and hanged upon it for my sins and my wicked doings. Also as I *mused* upon this His progress, that Scripture dropped upon my spirit — He was ordained to the slaughter.' My brethren, to read about your Saviour in that *seeing* way is the whole secret. Only *see* what you read about, and hear about, and sing about, and pray about, and preach about, and all the rest will follow. Your eye, like the prophet's eye, will always affect your heart. And when your heart is properly and sufficiently affected that will soon drive all the idleness out of all your words, till all you think, and all you say, and all you do will be well-pleasing in the sight of God. And what a reward that will be!

So much on reading Holy Scripture in that idleness-dispersing way. Now just for a moment take the praise of God in the same way. And we cannot take a better example for our purpose than that heavenly hymn, ' Rock of Ages, cleft for me.' For that hymn is both prayer and praise of the first order. Now to-night just repeat or chant to yourselves ' Rock of Ages,' with your eye all the time on the Object, that is to say on Christ crucified for you. That is to say doing the thing all the time you are saying or singing the words. As thus: cleft for me! Always as you utter the great words think you are standing on Mount Calvary and are looking on Christ actually being crucified on that cross for you. *See* Him and come up close to Him, and as if there were no one near Him but you, say to Him: Let me hide myself in Thee! Let me hide myself in Thee from all my past sins, from all my present temptations of all kinds and of all degrees, and even from my evil and unseemly self. Look up and say to Him—Nothing in my hands I bring, simply to Thy cross I cling. And let that not be an idle word in such a place and at such a moment. But throw your arms around His bleeding Body, and so hide yourself for ever in His sin-atoning and debt-discharging sacrifice. And so on as the Spirit of God and your own believing heart will teach you to the end of your great hymn of Christ-appropriating praise. Do that once to-night and you will feel such a sense of reality and truth and power that you will sing in the same way all your days. And that not only with that heavenly hymn but with all the psalms and hymns and spiritual songs that have hitherto been such a tissue of idle words to you. Always sing with your eye on the Divine Object and your eye will infallibly both satisfy and sanctify your heart.

Intercessory prayer is not seldom a very idle and a very unprofitable performance even when it is performed at all. For how often our friends

in their distress ask us to pray for them and how
seldom we do it to any purpose! I wonder if I
can venture to tell you what is in my mind about
intercessory prayer at this moment. I wonder if
I dare tell you, I wonder if it would be wise to
speak, as I feel compelled to speak, to such a
mixed multitude as you are. Yes I will venture
and will risk. For I am debtor to all the devout
and serious-minded people among you with a
debt I can never fully discharge. And then, who
knows, but it may be the same with some of you
some day as it was with me. Well, a dear friend
of mine was sick and was seemingly nigh unto
death. And I was much in prayer for him that
he might be spared to his family and to his
friends and to his great work. And one night
as I was in that intercessory prayer a Voice
suddenly spake and said to me—'Are you in
real earnest in what you ask? Or are you utter-
ing, as usual, so many of your idle words in this
solemn matter? Now to prove the sincerity and
the integrity of your love for your friend, and
to seal the truth of what you say about the
value of his life, will you give Me and yourself a
solid proof that you are in real earnest in what
you say?' 'What is the proof?' I asked, all
trembling, and without looking up. And the
Voice said, 'Will you consent to transfer to your
sick friend the half of your remaining years?
Suppose you have two more years to live and
work yourself, will you give over one of them to
your friend? Or if you have ten years yet before

you, will you let your friend have five of them ?'
I sprang to my feet in a torrent of sweat. It
was a kind of garden of Gethsemane to me.
But, like Gethsemane, I got strength to say,
'Let it be as Thou hast said. Thy will be done.
Not my will but Thine be done.' Till I lay
down that never-to-be-forgotten night with a
clean heart and a good conscience as never before
both toward God and toward my much-talented
friend. How the matter is to end I know not.
How the case is to work out I cannot tell.
Enough for me and for you that my story is
true and is no idle tale.

VIII

'I DID NOT REMEMBER THE SINS OF MY YOUTH; NAY, THE SINS OF ONE DAY I FORGOT THE NEXT DAY'

FORGETFUL GREEN was the most dangerous spot in all the way up to the Celestial City. 'Your father,' said Greatheart to Samuel, 'had that sorest battle of his at a place yonder before us in a narrow passage just beside Forgetful Green. And it is always so,' said the much-experienced guide. 'For if at any time any man meets with any severe brunt it is when he forgets what favours he has received from God and how utterly unworthy he is of those favours.' So far the famous guide to Samuel the son of Christian the pilgrim.

And now first for doctrine, and then after that for application—as the great Puritan preachers were wont to lay down their discourses. Well, the doctrine here is this: Great sins forgiven must never be forgotten. For when any man begins to forget his past sins, as a consequence he soon begins to forget his Saviour and everything else of that kind. And in order that that disastrous state of matters may not come to any of His true people God as a rule works in them a deeply penitential mind : and that not only when their sins are first committed, but He most graciously continues that mind in them, aye and sometimes greatly increases it, long after those past sins of theirs have been confessed and forgiven and forsaken. In the spiritual experience of many a forgiven sinner the old guilt with a new contrition on account of that guilt will on occasion return and that again and again. And Job, as well as many more Bible saints, were often brought in by those masterly experimental preachers as so many proofs of that. As one of the best of those preachers has it : 'God's great servant Job, for the sins of his youth, for which, questionless, he had often humbled himself, yet did God, for His own purposes, write bitter things against that saint many years after, and did make him to old age still to possess the sins of his youth.' And he continues : 'In our stupidity, and in our presumption, we think that the mere lapse of the years somehow wears out both the great guilt of our long past sins, as well as weakens God's demand on us for a broken heart on account of those sins. We think so. But it is not so. It is very far from being so. Great sins forgiven must never for a single day be forgotten.' So far Thomas Goodwin.

Now if that is sound doctrine, as undeniably it is, then it follows that we must all our life long believe it and practise it. That is to say we must continually revisit our past lives, so as to keep our present minds penitent and our present hearts broken. And in doing so we shall be working together with God who turns all our past life, sins and all, as well as all our present life, sinfulness and all, to our everlasting salvation and to His own everlasting glory. The great preacher from whom I have borrowed above was wont in his own words, ' to take a turn up and down in his past life ' every Sabbath morning, and that penitential practice of his made him to be the great evangelical preacher he was in Oxford to over eighty years of age. And no man who has any at all of the true teaching and the true leading of God's Holy Spirit in these personal matters, no such man can look back on his past life without a multitude of heart-breaking things rushing in upon him. Small minds, and coarse minds, and pharisaic minds can think only of gross sins, as they are called. But when God selects and sets apart any great sinner for a great sanctification, there is no end to the humiliations and the contritions that come to that sinful man, and that out of things and out of circumstances that another man would count of no importance at all. And this same way of God's universal working has given us some of the most precious passages in the prophets, and in the psalmists, and in the apostles, as well as in our best spiritual literature, as every well-read man knows.

There is one far too common sin of the days of our youth that some men, I fear, will not admit to be a sin at all. But by whatever name you call that sin, its wages and its fruits are not seldom death sooner or later, and that sometimes to both parties. The days of our youth are the days of our ' love-making ' as we call it. And the apostle has a most suggestive expression that comes in most fitly at this point. Paul speaks again and again of ' love unfeigned.' Now some young men feign love, and make love, as the saying is, when they do not as yet feel it. They indulge themselves in feigning love till the time comes when they both feel and confess to a true love. They feign love in their looks and in their words and in their actions till others are deceived by all that and think them and take them to be in earnest. ' It may be sport to you,' said the ill-used creatures in Æsop, ' but it is death to us.' Young men, be men! Be Christian gentlemen! And study to do to other men's daughters, and to other men's sisters, and to other men's future wives as you would have other young men do to your daughters, and to your sisters, and to your future wives. A word is enough to the wise.

And now from that let us go on to look at some of God's ways of recalling their past sins to such of His people as are under His special sanctification. For when any of his more chosen

people begin to forget their past sins He has
many ways at His command of bringing back
their past to their painful and penitential re-
membrance : many ways. There are special men
of His among ourselves—I could give you some
of their names—sorely beset men of His whom
He handles in this way, as they will testify to
you till you could scarcely believe that they are
in their sober senses. If they would but speak
out to you and could trust you they would tell
you that they never so much as open their letters
of a morning, or lift their newspaper, or cross
their door-step, or walk along the street, or pass
that door and that window, or enter a railway
carriage and pass that station and that bridge
and that stream and see that far-away farm-
house up on the side of that hill, without their
sanctification taking another start forward.
Some long-past sin, some long-past wrong done
or suffered, some long-past cruelty perpetrated
or endured, some long-past love not unfeigned,
some never-to-be-forgotten trespass against God
and man and woman, some print set on the heels
of their feet, some old sore set a-running in
their conscience. The old-world tragedians were
wont on the stage to teach the people that if
you take a murderer into the presence of a
murdered corpse the cold and closed wounds
in that murdered corpse will immediately open
again and will begin to run hot blood again, as
much as to point to the murderer and say—
Thou art the man ! And so it is with a sinner's

conscience. Bring his guilty conscience within a thousand miles of the scene of his sin and he will think every bush an officer. Till all the other prisoners will overhear him singing in the night watches, and saying, ' Rock of Ages ! cleft for me, let me hide myself in Thee !' And till he comes day and night, and all his days on earth, to exclaim with John Bunyan : ' O Christ ! O Christ ! O Christ ! Thou Saviour so suitable for me !'

'When my God left me to myself,' says Shepard, 'I forgot the sins of my youth ; nay, worse than even that, the sins of one day I forgot the next day.' With all his fulness in some places Shepard does not dwell at any length upon that in his extant diary. But a far better writer does. You will all remember what the author of the *Serious Call* did to himself to make himself to remember the sins of every newly past day. You will all remember how he was wont to pray at the third hour of every returning day for the grace of humility, and at the sixth hour of every new day for more and more love in his heart to God and man, and then at the ninth hour of every departing day for immediate and entire resignation to the will of God in everything. And then you will remember how that so able and so sincere and so honest man always sequestered himself at night and took himself over the past day, and especially over the use he had made of the humility and the love and the resignation he had so pointedly prayed for. And that so

punctual and so searching self-examination of his
led him sometimes to a great sacrifice of praise
the last thing that night. But sometimes and
not seldom he was compelled to offer that other
sacrifice that we are assured so greatly pleases
God—a broken spirit, a broken and a contrite
heart. And then the next morning he wakened
himself up early by saying: 'When I awake I
am still with Thee!' And then both the successes
and the defeats of yesterday made him both
watch and pray and obey all the better every
new day. Now in that same way take your
own yesterday yourselves. Well, what sort of a
day was yesterday with you? Was it a good day
or was it an undeniably bad day? It was so I
have good reason to know with one of you. But
our very worst days are sometimes turned into
our best days, as it was with some of us yesterday. And indeed it is always so with all those
men among us who are truly under the grace
and under the Spirit of God. The worse their
day is the more they take out of it before they
sleep; the more repentance they take out of it,
the more humility, the more resignation, the
more despair of themselves, the more true prayer,
and the more true faith in their Lord and Saviour
Jesus Christ: in His blood to cleanse, in His
righteousness to justify, and in His Spirit to
sanctify. And all that not in idle words, as is the
case with most men among us, but all that to an
experimental reality that quiets the most exasperated conscience and heals the most broken heart.

F

Now before you go down from God's house to your own house I have a golden word from God to all of you who constantly bewail and bemoan your bad past and refuse to be comforted concerning it. A thousand of the most honoured saints of God in Holy Scripture and in the Church of Christ down to our own day, all rise up around you and claim a right and indeed have a divine commission to comfort you. And they will all tell you that never, no never, were a penitent man's past sins permitted to prejudice either his future saintliness or his future service. The biographies and the autobiographies and the spiritual experiences of God's greatest saints were not written for their sakes alone, but for your sake also, if only you will read them aright and enough. Read aright then about Noah, and about Jacob, and about Moses, and about David, and about Isaiah, and about Peter, and about Paul, and indeed about all the men whose names are most dear to the Church of Christ. And if you read about them aright and enough; that is to say, so as to take heart of faith and hope out of them for yourselves; then one day your names also will be added to that long and shining Roll. As you have imitated those men so well in your life of sin, go on now and henceforth to imitate them in your life of repentance and faith and true Gospel holiness, and your names also will yet be found written in heaven in the golden Roll of God's elect and Christ's redeemed. Believe it and you shall certainly see it. Believe it boldly and with full assurance of faith and it shall certainly be to you according to your faith. For your faith is to you, in this matter also, the substance of the things you hope for, and it is the evidence to you of things not seen by you as yet. Therefore, continually repent of your past and continually believe the Gospel. Live and die believing the Gospel.

IX

'I LEARNED FROM THE APOSTLE HOW TO COMPARE SPIRITUAL THINGS WITH SPIRITUAL'

EVERY truly original writer has had to create his own vocabulary. Every truly great and every truly original writer has made such new discoveries in truth, or he has taken such new and original views of some old truth, or he has had such new and original experiences of life that he has been compelled to construct a new language for himself in order that he might somewhat adequately set forth to his readers his great discoveries and his great experiences.

Now no greater nor more original writer has ever lived than the Apostle Paul. Take Paul's great natural powers, and then take the great revelations that were made to him, and then take his own unparalleled experiences, and Paul stands alone among all the great and original men who have ever opened a mouth to speak to us or have taken up a pen to write to us. No other writer or preacher has ever had such new things and such deep things to deal with, and accordingly it is not at all to be wondered at that he has a terminology in all his epistles that is both absolutely new and absolutely his own. The Apostle was raised up to be the author of an absolutely new theology and an absolutely new anthropology and an absolutely new philosophy and an absolutely new ethic, and all that compelled him to be the creator of an absolutely new vocabulary. Incomparably rich as the Greek language was in its philosophical and ethical and literary terms, at the same time when Paul took up his pen to write to his converts in Corinth concerning their Divine Redeemer and concerning the intellectual and spiritual riches of their redemption, he was compelled to employ, not the words which man's wisdom teacheth, but the words which the Holy Spirit teacheth, comparing spiritual things with spiritual.

Now there is no single word in the whole of the Apostle's vocabulary that has undergone such a deepening and such an exalting and such an enriching process as just this word 'spiritual' in the text. Paul did not literally coin this word spiritual. He found it already in existence in his Greek dictionary and he was quite familiar with it in the best Greek literature. He did not actually create this word spiritual but he did better. For he took it up and rescued it from all its physical and even from all its philosophical associations, and he exalted it and ennobled it and glorified it and made it one of

the deepest and sweetest most holy and most
heavenly words in all our New Testament terminology.   Before Paul so took up and so trans-
figured this word it merely meant the immaterial
soul or spirit of man as distinguished from his
material body.   But in his transforming hands
the word was at once lifted up above all its
former associations till it became ever after one
of the noblest and sweetest of all the words
belonging to the Spirit of God and to His
spiritual world.   Says Jonathan Edwards in his
great chapter on this subject : ' Spiritual in Paul
is no longer used to denote anything connected
with the soul or spirit of man.   In Paul qualities
are not said to be spiritual because they have
their seat in the soul and not in the body.   But
it is solely with relation to the Holy Spirit, the
Third Person in the Godhead, that either persons
or things are termed spiritual in Paul.   The
Holy Spirit is the substantive,' says that great
writer, ' from which Paul forms and fills up
his great adjective spiritual.   Christian men,'
Edwards adds, ' are described by Paul as spiritual
men because they are born of the Spirit of God,
and because the Spirit of God dwells and works
within them.'

PRIMA SPIRITUALIA was a theological expression
much made use of by the deep old divines.   They
described God the Father and God the Son and
God the Holy Ghost, when viewed in their divine
holiness, as the PRIMA SPIRITUALIA—that is to
say the Three Divine Persons are the first and

they are the best of all Spiritual Existences. In
the Three Divine Persons we have spirituality in
summo gradu as those old masters in Israel said.
So transcendent is the Divine spirituality, said
those masterly men, that we cannot attain to
think aright about it, not to speak of comparing
ourselves with it even at our spiritually best.
But when God the Son humbled Himself and
became the Son of Man, by that stupendous
descent He brought down the Divine spirituality
somewhat to our level, so to speak. Till we can
now both intelligently and reverently compare
ourselves with Him, incomparably as He is above
us. We can now measure ourselves, so to speak,
over against Him, immeasurably as He will always
excel us in His spirituality as in everything else.
For as John has it: ' The Word was made flesh
and dwelt among us, and we beheld His glory,
the glory as of the Only-Begotten of the Father,
full of grace and truth. And of His fulness have
all we received, and grace for grace.' That is to
say, we have received grace somewhat corresponding to His grace till we can now in some not
untrue sense compare our graces with His graces.
Look then at some of His incarnation graces.
As the evangelical prophet has them, ' The Spirit
of the LORD shall rest upon Him, the spirit of
wisdom and understanding, the spirit of counsel
and might, the spirit of knowledge, and of the
fear of the LORD. And righteousness shall be the
girdle of His loins, and faithfulness the girdle
of His reins.' As He said of Himself in the

synagogue at Nazareth : 'The Spirit of the LORD
God is upon me, because He hath anointed me
to preach the gospel to the poor; He hath sent
me to heal the broken-hearted : to preach deliverance to the captives and the recovering of
sight to the blind, and to set at liberty them
that are bruised.' And then all His after-life on
earth was one long and unbroken revelation of
the profound spirituality of His heart and His
character. Till one who had been with Him
from the beginning, and had walked with Him
and watched Him every day, was able to stake
his life on this testimony concerning his Master,
that ' He did no sin, neither was guile found in
His mouth. Who, when He was reviled reviled
not again; when He suffered He threatened not :
but committed Himself to Him that judgeth
righteously.' And this life went on with Him
till all the fruits of the Spirit were found in all
their richness and ripeness in Him—that is to
say all love, and all joy, and all peace, and all
long-suffering, and all gentleness, and all goodness, and all faith, and all meekness, and all
temperance of every kind. In short all those
spiritual things in which we are able to compare
ourselves with Him. Now with us, as with
Shepard, how do we compare in all these things
with Him who is our example and our standard ?
When we are reviled, what do we do ? When
men accuse us falsely, what do we do ? When
we suffer wrongfully, what do we do ? Do we
love and wish well to the man who is our enemy ?

Are we peacemakers in our churches and in our families and in our civil communities? And what about our meekness and our humility which were our Lord's special and favourite graces? Let us lay our lives alongside of our Lord's life, and so compare ourselves with Him till we become spiritual with His spirituality, and thus everlastingly blessed with His everlasting blessedness.

'The law is spiritual,' says the Apostle in his great autobiographic chapter, 'but I am carnal, sold under sin.' Paul had held his head high till the spirituality of God's law took hold of his heart. But as soon as the spirituality and true holiness of the law entered his heart, in his own words he died. If his head was the highest before no other man's head ever since has been so low as Paul's head. All spiritually-minded men, and all men who would fain possess a spiritual mind, should study Paul's autobiography down to the bottom, and till they see themselves in it as in a glass. We have many autobiographies, first and last, and some of them are more to us than much fine gold. But Paul's autobiography was the first of its kind and it remains the best of its kind to this day. It is so short. It is so succinct. It is so profound. It is so spiritual. It is so evangelical. And it has saved so many spiritually-minded men in all ages from downright despair. Do not neglect the Apostle's peerless autobiography but compare your own with it continually; comparing spiritual things with spiritual.

'I was no longer an infidel,' writes John Newton in his *Authentic Autobiography*. 'I heartily renounced all my former profaneness. I was truly sorry for my past life, and I purposed an immediate amendment. Thus, to all appearance, I was a new man. But, alas! I was little aware of the innate evils of my own heart. For I had no apprehension at all of the spirituality, that is to say, the length and the breadth and the height and depth of the law of God. And though I began to inquire after spiritual books, yet having no spiritual discernment, I frequently made a wrong choice in my religious reading. And I was not yet brought in the way of evangelical and spiritual preaching, and what I heard of that kind I understood not.' Now whole multitudes of men and women in all our churches are exactly like John Newton in this matter of their religious reading. Multitudes have an intellectual and a scholarly and an artistic discernment in the matter of books who have absolutely no spiritual discernment at all in that whole region of things. How few of the religious books of our day would please the Apostle, or even Shepard! Almost any book passes muster among our people for a spiritual book if only it has some quasi-religious words on its title-page and some thin flavour of religiosity hanging about its boards. Now amid such a widespread and disastrous lack of intellectual and spiritual discernment what exactly is a spiritual book? Well, a book is spiritual to please Paul and Shepard

and Newton and the deep old divines just in the
measure that the PRIMA SPIRITUALIA are to be
seen in it—that is to say, just in the measure
that the Father and the Son and the Holy Ghost
are in it, and are in it in all their spirituality.
And the Father is seen in all His spirituality
only when He is seen and rejoiced in as blessing
us with all spiritual blessings in heavenly places
in Christ Jesus His Son. Blessing us with all
such spiritual blessings as our election in Christ
to be holy and without blame before God is love,
as the spiritually-minded Apostle has it in his so
spiritual Epistle to the Ephesians. As also our
having our redemption through the blood of
Christ and the forgiveness of our sins according
to the riches of His grace. And then following
the Father's so spiritual part in our salvation
there is the Son's so spiritual part, and then the
so spiritual part of Him from whose Divine Nature
and Divine Work we get the word spiritual and
all that it connotes and all that it conveys. These
are the things that make a book spiritual;
spiritual and evangelical. And without these all-
essential things a religious book may be widely
sold and bought among us; it may be loudly
praised and widely read among us; but lacking
the PRIMA SPIRITUALIA it can never satisfy a
reader of real intellectual and spiritual discernment. 'I frequently made a wrong choice in my
religious reading,' says the future author of that
spiritual masterpiece, *The Cardiphonia.* Indeed,
he never made a right choice of a religious book

nor could he till he both received and exercised that spiritual discernment in the matter of books which is one of the most enriching of the gifts of the Spirit to the mind and the heart of a mature spiritual man. Pray God the 'Holy Ghost for that discernment in your buying and in your reading of books, and conscientiously exercise that discernment when you once get it. Do so lest Brutus should rise up in the day of judgment to condemn you. For it is written concerning the great stoic that he never read a book but to make himself a better man. What have you to say to that, O you so-called Christian men and women?

But there is one thing more on which a closing word claims to be said. And that word is this. In what is in some respects the greatest chapter the Apostle Paul ever wrote he lays down this absolute and irreversible law of God that 'to be carnally minded is death, but to be spiritually minded is life and peace.' Now, from your own experience you will at once subscribe to the first part of that strong statement. For your own carnal mind has many and many a time been nothing short of death to you. But the second statement must often have staggered and confounded you: this statement, namely, that to be spiritually minded is life and peace. And no wonder that you are so staggered and confounded with that. For the truth is, both to Paul himself and to you, the very opposite has been the

indisputable case. Like Paul himself, you had
life and peace both with God and with yourself
till God's spiritual law truly entered your mind
and your heart. 'I had not known sin,' you
have said a thousand times in the bitterness of
your heart, ' but by God's holy law, for I had
not known envy and covetousness and a lascivious
mind in myself unless God's holy law had entered
and had denounced all these things in me. I
was alive, I was light-minded and light-hearted
as long as I kept God's holy law outside of my
mind and my heart,' you say, ' but when that
holy law came home to me, I died.' That is to
say, ever since you saw the heart-searching
spirituality and the awful holiness of the law
of God you have been in an inward misery that
makes you sometimes the very wretchedest of
men, Paul and you. Now what can Paul pos-
sibly mean when he says that to have such a
spiritualised mind is life and peace, when, in his
own experience and in yours it is the very
opposite ? He means this. He means take pure
and unopposed spirituality of mind in any man,
if such a man could be found, and both life and
peace of the most perfect kind will always
be found in that man, as surely as such life
and peace were always found in Jesus Christ
Himself. But neither Paul nor you are as
yet that happy man. For in Paul and in
you, in the meantime, your hearts remain
largely carnal even after your minds have become largely spiritual. You are like those

pitiable Galatians, just as Paul was so like them himself.

'I learned from Paul,' says Shepard, 'what it was to be spiritually-minded, and I learned from him also how to compare spiritual things with spiritual.'

X

'I CAME TO SEE HOW GOD IS HAVING HIS NAME IN ME'

S I was reading Thomas Shepard to myself one night last week I came again and again on this striking exclamation, 'O! the reason is God will have His Name.' That great experimental divine is dwelling with deep spiritual insight on some of God's more mysteri ous ways with some men. As for instance his so intricate and past-finding-out providences with some men, His so extraordinary and so unaccountable goodness and grace to some men, His so marvellous loving-kindness and tender-mercy to some men, His so immeasurable and amazing long-suffering with some men, and so on. And then that great experimental preacher exclaims, 'O! the reason is that God will have His Name.'

Well then to begin with, what is His Name? My brethren, it is our best happiness on earth that we do not need to ask that question. For there is nothing that we know so well as just the Name of the Lord. The Name of the Lord is our best and our most cherished knowledge. It is our present and our everlasting salvation. The Name of the Lord is the sure ground of all our hope for time and eternity. For it is this: 'The Lord: the Lord God; merciful and gracious, long-suffering, and abundant in goodness and truth: forgiving iniquity, transgression, and sin.'

Now if that is the Divinely-declared Name of the Lord what exactly is it for Him to 'have His Name' according to that striking expression of His servant? It is this. It is to have His Name proclaimed and published and manifested to all men and to all time as He Himself proclaimed and manifested His Name to Moses on the Mount. And it is to have His Name listened to and understood and received and appropriated and rested on and feared and loved and adored and glorified—and all that by all believing men. Now not only the thirty-fourth of Exodus but the whole Bible from Genesis to Revelation is full of the Name of the Lord. The Name of the Lord: and then all the ways He has taken in order to 'have His Name': that is what 'the Scriptures principally teach.' And that is what our own lives principally teach as soon and as often as we begin to read our own lives in the light of His Name.

Take to begin with some of God's more special and more personal providences towards some men. For there are some men who by reason of God's special and peculiar providences toward them

give Him back His Name every day. His providences toward them are such that they are
compelled to take refuge in His Name actually
every hour of every day. Their very first thought
every new morning has to be the Name of the
Lord. The Name of the Lord repeated to themselves as they rise off their bed is more to them
than their morning clothing and their morning
meal. But for their recollection of the Name of
the Lord they could not face the coming day,
and far less could they face the recollection and
the review of the departed day. And all the day
it is the same experience with them. The returning day would simply be impossible to them, were
it not for the Name of the Lord. They make
haste like Moses and bow their head and worship
a hundred times every day. Dear old Jacob
Behmen told a much-tempted disciple of his to
throw himself every half-hour into the abyss of
the Divine Name, and he would get strength
there that would enable him to live out of reach
of all the sins and all the miseries and all the
crosses and all the tribulations of which his life
was full. And there are men among ourselves
exactly like the Teutonic philosopher and his
much-tried disciple. Sudden providences, unfore-
seen providences, unexpected and unprepared-for
providences, rush in every hour of every day
upon some men. A word suddenly falls on
their ears, an image suddenly falls on their eyes,
a thought suddenly arises in their minds, a feeling suddenly awakens in their hearts, and that

G

moment God has His Name again in those men.
They flee every moment they live to the Name
of the LORD as a bird flees to its mountain. To
those men their life is a daily miracle. It is a
miracle to them how their life is beset before
and behind and is surrounded unceasingly with
special providences and secret visitations that all
work together to give God His Name! They
have never heard nor read anywhere such a work
of divine wonder as their own life is. Till they
come to see that nothing less than the whole
Name of the LORD is the real meaning and the
true end of their whole life in this world. Any
other explanation of their life falls far short of
the facts. Till they can accept no other theory
of their life but that the Lord is having His
whole Name adorned in them as He is having it
adorned in no other man they know or have ever
heard of. Says Shepard on this subject: ' You
shall find this if the Lord for His Name sake
loves thee, there is not any carriage or passage of
His providence toward thee but He gets Himself
His name by means of it. For if this be God's
end, every passage of His providence is but a
means to this end.'

But there is one thing in your life that is far
more mysterious and far more staggering and far
more cross-bearing to some of you than your
most mysterious and perplexing and cross-bearing providences; and that is your so prolonged
and so postponed sanctification; your unattained
and seemingly unattainable holiness of heart and

life. And you are not alone in that, though you often think you are. Their slow, standstill, back-going sanctification has been the most staggering of all the staggering experiences of God's best saints from the beginning of His saints till now, just as it has been the most perplexing problem that He has set His deepest preachers, such as Shepard, to deal with before their fit people; this profound problem—Why so much sinfulness is still left to pollute and to fester and to spread death and hell in the heart and in the mind and in the life of the truly regenerate man? Well, God alone fully knows His own mind and His whole mind in all these matters. But I think I have somewhat of His mind when I say to you that all this is permitted, and indeed is ordained, in order that He may have His whole Name in you : His whole glorious and everlasting Name. God did not sanctify you on the same day on which He justified you. And that was so because He got His Name sufficiently, for one day, on that great day when He justified such an ungodly man as you are. Sufficient for one day was your first forgiveness. I will put it to yourself to say —If you had been both called and justified and adopted and sanctified wholly and all at once you would never have known, you would never have believed, what an inveterate and hopeless and unparalleled sinner you are, nor what a glorious Saviour you have got in the Son of God. No; it is not your first pardon that gives God His great Name in you. It is His every day and every hour pardon of your sins; sins that are past all name and past all belief. And that going on between God and you for a long lifetime of seventy or eighty years. And thus it is that God is getting and is going to get His great Name in you, such a Name as He has not got in Moses or in David or in Paul, great as His Name has been in them. And this goes on till under the agony of His Name in you the cry goes up from your ever-broken heart, the cry of the Psalmist and the Apostle: 'For Thy sake, O God, we are killed all the day long: we are accounted as sheep for the slaughter.' And till you sing with John Newton and say:

> I asked the Lord that I might grow
>   In faith, and love, and every grace;
> Might more of His salvation know,
>   And seek more earnestly His face.

> .   .   .   .

> Lord, why is this? I trembling cried,
>   Wilt Thou pursue a worm to death?
> ' 'Tis in this way,' the Lord replied,
>   ' I answer prayer for grace and faith.

> ' These inward trials I employ,
>   From self and pride to set thee free;
> And break thy schemes of earthly joy,
>   That thou mayest seek thy all in Me.'

In other words it was all in order that God might have His whole Name in the author of the *Olney Hymns*, and the *Cardiphonia*, and the *Authentic Narrative*, and in you and in me.

But more than all that, and far more wonder-

ful than all that—out of the greatest sins and
trespasses of His own redeemed and pardoned
people God gets by far His greatest Name. ' I
am not afraid,' says the greatest theologian of
the English Church : ' I am not afraid to affirm
it boldly, with St. Augustine, that men puffed
up through a proud opinion of themselves receive a great benefit at the hands of God when
they are permitted and that grievously to trans-
gress. . . . Ask the very soul of Peter, and it
shall undoubtedly make you this answer : " My
eager protestations, made in the glory of my
ghostly strength, I am ashamed of : but those
crystal tears, wherewith my sin and weakness
were bewailed, have procured my endless joy : my
strength was my ruin, but my fall has been
my stay." ' And our author, a divine of a very
different school as we say, agrees with Hooker
and almost surpasses him when he says : ' Hence
you shall find that those very sins that so dishonour His Name, He will even by them get
Himself a glorious Name : for He will be so far
from casting thee out of His love because of them
that He will do thee good by means of them.
Thy sins, that might well have been thy damna-
tion, He will make use of them to humble thee,
and to empty thee, for thy salvation. Doth not
thy weakness strengthen thee, like Paul ? Doth
not thy darkness make thee cry the more for
light, like David ? Do not thy falls into sin
make thee to be weary of sin, and to be watchful
against it, and full of longing to be for ever free

of it? And hence holy Mr. Fox has said that for
his part he thanked God for his sins far more
than for his good works.   O! the reason is that
God will have His whole Name.'   Paul was not
deterred from telling these deep truths in his
Epistle.   No not even by the fear that some of
his Roman readers would make a bad use of
them; and neither has judicious Hooker been
deterred, nor experimental Shepard, nor holy Mr.
Fox as you see and hear.

Now to sum all that up for ourselves this communion morning: God is such and His Name is
such that a multitude which no man can number
will all be needed—to let Him have His whole
Name from among them.   Every one of that
great multitude will in the end make his own
personal and peculiar contribution to the glory
of God's Name.   But it is your peculiar contribution that He is seeking here and now on this
communion day.   You say—some of you—that
there is not the like of you, you feel sure, in all
that redeemed and rejoicing multitude now before
the throne.   And God agrees with you in that.
He sees no one else at all like you among all His
elect.   And thus it is that He has His eye and
His heart so specially set upon you this communion morning.   He sees the prospect of His
Name in you as in no one else in all this house.
When he comes in immediately to see the guests
His eye will fall on you first.   For there are
things in the text that no one at the Table this
morning aright understands but yourself.   There

are things in His great Name that no one now
present will be able to draw out and adorn : no
one but you. The very things in your case that
make your case so extraordinary and so unparalleled are the sure and certain marks of your
special election to know and to show forth His
Covenant Name. 'In one sense,' says John
Newton in his golden *Cardiphonia* : 'In one
sense we are excellently well suited to answer
His eternal purpose. If we were not vile and
worthless beyond all expression, the exceeding
riches of His grace would not have been so glori-
ously displayed in us. His glory shines far more
in redeeming one sinner like you and me, than in
preserving and upholding a thousand angels like
Gabriel and Michael themselves.' Well then, if
all that is so, come away and make your special
and peculiar contribution to God's great Name.
Come away and contribute your abounding sinfulness, and God will contribute His still more
abounding grace and mercy. And God and you
working together in that way He will have His
whole and full Name in you, and that as in no
one else at the Table to-day, no, nor at the Table
above.

XI

'FOR THY SAKE I AM KILLED ALL THE DAY LONG, I AM ACCOUNTED AS A SHEEP FOR THE SLAUGHTER'

DEAN CHURCH says somewhere that what distinguished Dr. Newman's preaching above everything else was his wonderful power of realising and of making his hearers realise the truth of what he was saying. And it was this great gift of a realising imagination, even more than his magical style, that made Dr. Newman the matchless and the epoch-making preacher that he was: so his much-admiring friend assures us. Now, in all my life-long reading of those spiritual writers who themselves realise and who consequently make their readers realise the things of the spiritual life, I have never met with a more pungently realising writer than the founder of Harvard. And in proof of that, and in illustration of that, take for one thing the way he realised how he was literally slain to death every returning Sabbath day. 'Sabbath, August 16. Four things have slain my soul before God all

this day : the poverty of my provision for my
people, the felt unprofitableness of it all as I
delivered it, the utter deadness of heart that has
lain upon me all the day, and no true presence
of God with me in any part of my work.' On
the very next Sabbath he was even worse : ' I feel
that I deserve death and hell for the motives and
the intentions and the ambitions with which I
do my pulpit work.' Another Sabbath as he
rested on his bed between sermons he saw himself to be ' vile beyond all description.' They
are his own bitterly realising words : ' Vile beyond
all description, not because of any of the sins of
the flesh, but because of the infinitely worse sins
of the spirit. How could the God of holiness
ever make use of a sinful wretch like me ! He
could not, and I need not expect it.' Another
Sabbath as he vainly tried to take some rest at
the same hour a thousand things simply tortured
him. ' In whose name and in whose strength
and to whose glory did I do my work this morning ? I preached and prayed as with wings when
I got on well. I had great liberty and, as I
thought great spiritual joy as I repeated in my
prayers and in my sermons the eloquent passages
I had prepared with such labour beforehand.'
And all that rose before him with such shame
and pain that his bed swam under him with his
tears of remorse and misery. Another Sabbath
he was not well and a neighbour minister took
his pulpit. ' My wife came home praising above
measure Mr. T. H., his sermon. Oh, my God,

pity me with this diabolical heart of mine. For
all the time T. H. is my best friend.' Till he
quite forgot his bodily illness that day in the far
worse illness of his soul. 'November 16. I felt
my heart all day to be very unsavoury. I was
full of darkness and death. And I felt sometimes as if I were already on my bed in hell.
And I saw as never before that nothing but free
grace and that abounding toward me could help
me out of my exceeding sinfulness, and on that
grace alone did I hang my heart all that day.'
And if you are not dead tired of such a monster
of a minister as Shepard, take this one more
entry of his : 'December 9. After my Wednesday
sermon I saw the towering pride of my heart in
all I did. As soon as I had done any public
work my wicked heart would immediately look
wistfully whether men praised me enough or no.
Hereupon I saw my incurable vileness to make
the opinions of passing men my rule and my stay
and my reward in doing the work of the everlasting God. I saw also that upon every enlargement of mine I was ready to be somewhat in my
own eyes. Whereupon my rule now is to be
more vile than any other man in my own eyes,
and that every day. For Thy sake I am killed
all the day. I am accounted as a sheep for
the slaughter.' 'The saints are lowered,' sings
Newman, 'that the world may rise.'

But with all that, what can this so startling
scripture mean when it says, ' *For Thy sake* we
are killed all the day long, and are accounted as

sheep for the slaughter'? And how are we to
realise all that in David, and in Paul and in his
Roman readers, and in Shepard and in his New
England readers, and most of all in ourselves?
How can it be said in any true and sober-minded
sense that it was 'for God's sake;' for any
advantage or pleasure to Him that Thomas
Shepard was so slaughtered in his soul on all
those so sinful Sabbath days? What conceivable
service could have been done to God by all those
shameful self-discoveries and self-condemnations
of His unsanctified servant? Much service, my
brethren, and that in many ways. And in this
way for one. 'Thou desirest truth in the inward
part, and in the hidden part Thou shalt make
me to know wisdom.' So writes David when,
like Shepard, he is undergoing a specially inward
and a specially spiritual sanctification. That is
to say, God is first and foremost to David and
to Shepard the God of truth, and as such He
demands and He will have the whole truth about
themselves from all His elect servants, however
terrible that truth may be. And indeed the
more terrible that truth is the more He demands
it, and the more He will have it at any cost to
His servants and to Himself. And thus it is literally and really and supremely for His sake, and
for the sake of His truth and His holiness, that
His choicest servants have their eyes so opened
to see the whole of the awful truth about themselves. Yes, blessed be His gracious name for
ever. Almighty God accounts it His highest

glory, He holds it as all done for His special sake, when we come to Him in our uttermost misery and cast ourselves at His feet to redeem us and to save us. Poor Thomas Shepard's puffed-up heart when he was praised for a prayer or for a sermon, his utter prostration and desolation of heart when he did not receive the flattery for which he had laboured and looked, his heart-killing discernment of his miserable motives and intentions and ambitions in all he did and said in his study and in his pulpit and in his pastorate, his diabolical hatred of all the men who excelled him in their talents and in their attainments and in their popularity and in their prosperity, with all the rest of that awful book of his which he wrote out in secret and laid open before God, and which God has had put into our hands this evening—all that was suffered far less for Shepard's sake than for God's sake. All that was gone through by Shepard, and it was all written and is now all read in order that God might have His Name in Shepard, as he says himself in another powerful and pungent passage. We all read indeed that God's law is a spiritual law, and that all His commandments are holy and just and good. And again we read that the word of God is quick and powerful, and is sharper than any two-edged sword, piercing to the dividing asunder of soul and spirit, and is a discerner of the thoughts and intents of the heart. We read all that on occasion, and we do not in as many words deny the truth of it. But

we do not truly realise one single syllable of it
till we come to have it all experienced and
fulfilled and exhibited in our individual selves.
The whole heart-searching and heart-breaking
holiness of God's law could not be learned out
of mere texts of scripture however inspired and
however written out. God has not only to get
Holy Scripture written out and read and opened
up, but He has to get now one and now another
of His most gifted and most sanctified servants
killed by His holy law all the day long in order to
bring out and to illustrate and to teach to others
the heart-piercing and soul-saving spirituality of
His holy law. He has to get a David in one age,
and a Paul in another age, and a Luther in
another age, and a Shepard in another age, in
whose profound experience His holy law shall
have its free course and be magnified.

But while all that is so, at the same time
so manifold and so deep is the wisdom of God
that what is suffered by us supremely for His
sake is also suffered by us scarcely less supremely
for our own sake. As here, David was the
first who realised that it was for God's sake
that he was killed all the day long. Now when
we go back and read and realise David's much-
suffering psalm, we soon see that David's own
sake is as deeply involved in that psalm as is
God's sake. With all the untold suffering that
God and man are able to accumulate on David,
he is able and he is bold to call God to be his
witness in this way. Just listen to how David

is killed all the day long and with what results to himself. 'Thou hast cast me off and hast put me to shame. They which hate me spoil me for themselves. Thou hast given me like a sheep appointed for meat. Thou hast sold me for nought, and hast not increased Thy wealth by my price. Thou hast made me a reproach to my neighbours, and a scorn and a derision to those who are round about me. My confusion is continually before me, and the shame of my face hath covered me. All this is come upon me, yet have I not forgotten Thee, neither have I dealt falsely with Thy covenant. My heart is not turned back, nor have my steps declined from Thy way. For Thy sake I am killed all the day long. I am accounted as a sheep for the slaughter.' Now, all that daily slaughter of David was ordained of God in order that David's faith and trust and submissiveness and obedience might be exercised to their very utmost: might be exercised and manifested and perfected to their very utmost. And when Paul takes his Roman readers back to the forty-fourth Psalm it is in order that both he and they may imitate David in their faith and trust and submissiveness and obedience when they are killed all the day. And it was among the awful sufferings of the apostle's persecuted life that he was enabled to take to himself David's suffering and triumphant psalm and to realise it and to enrich it in this New Testament way. 'Who shall separate us from the love of Christ? Shall tribulation, or

distress, or persecution, or famine, or nakedness,
or peril, or sword ? Nay, in all these things we
are more than conquerors through Him that
loved us.' Now if all that is true of the outward
sufferings of the psalmist and the apostle, much
more splendidly is it true of their inward and
spiritual sufferings. You must all see how much
it was for David's own sake and for Paul's own
sake and for Shepard's own sake that they were
all three so inwardly killed all the day. To keep
to Shepard, you must all see how much it was for
his true sight of himself, and for his consequent
growth in saving grace, that he was so slaughtered
every returning Sabbath day. At any rate,
whether you see that or no, all your ministers
see it till they see little else. What minister
who reads or hears of Shepard's Sabbath night
entries does not immediately go to Shepard's
God in prayer for grace to see himself and to
despise and detest himself as that distinguished
saint did ? And what minister who has seen
himself as in a glass in Shepard will ever again
for a single Sabbath night forget what manner of
man he is ? Till this will be his secret and his
agonising cry to God all his Sabbaths on earth :
' For my own salvation's sake, O my God, kill
me in this way all my life long ! As long as
the remains of any such spiritual sin still dwells
in my heart, make me to die daily on account of
it, like David, and like Paul, and like that New
England Puritan of Thine. And I will bless the
day I ever heard his honoured name !' My

brethren, how wonderful, that what is so acutely suffered by God's servants is all suffered first and last for God's sake, but is also at the same time absolutely indispensable for their own sakes also. Till they make it their adoring cry continually : O the depth of the riches both of the wisdom and knowledge of God ! How unsearchable are His judgments, and His ways past finding out ! For who hath known the mind of the Lord ? or who hath been His counsellor ?

But with all that we are not come near the end of God's manifold wisdom in this deepest of all His dealings with His servants. For not only were Shepard's terrible sufferings undergone first for God's sake, and then after that for his own sake, but they were all ordained and overruled for our sake also. I say for our sake also. For had it not been for the terrible nature and the terrible amount of Shepard's spiritual sufferings we would never have so much as heard his name. Speaking for myself, it was the way he was killed every day, and it was specially the way he was absolutely slaughtered every Sabbath day, it was that which first drew me to this great saint for my spiritual profit and growth in grace. And still as I read and re-read the terrible diary of his soul I again see that great preacher and great pastor in the Divine making. He was one of the foremost students of Emmanuel College in Cambridge and all his days he kept up his studious habits. But it was neither his classical nor his theological scholarship that made him the great Puritan at whose feet I sit. It was his discovered sinfulness. He was like Luther. The devil was one of Shepard's most diligent and most successful tutors. It was Shepard's outward temptations, taken along with his inward corruptions, that made him the master in Israel that he is to some men among us. His books, I admit, are not spoonmeat. He does not write for babes at the breast. And that is why he has been so much neglected and forgotten even among the men of his own spiritual and ecclesiastical household. His *Parable* and his *Spiritual Experiences* are both written with his heart's blood, and it is this that makes those spiritual masterpieces so invaluable to those ministers, Puritan and other, who have sinfulness enough in their own hearts, and who have eyes enough alongside of that sinfulness, to enable them to read and to understand such masterly books, so full of intellectual and spiritual power: to read them continually and more and more to profit by them.

But I am forgetting. You are not sinful ministers and you do not need to be killed all the day long for the salvation of your people. No. But it will be no light discipline that will be needed to enable you to understand and to appreciate such ministers as are killed daily in order that their people may live. It will be no light discipline that you will need if you are to understand David in his forty-fourth Psalm, and Paul in his seventh and eighth of the Romans,

H

and Shepard in his *Spiritual Experiences*. But even though you are not ministers, and devoted to death like them, you are not on that account shut out from their great salvation. In your lay and retired life you may be as much killed every day for God's sake and for your own sake as any of your ministers are. Now, are you? For that is the point of this whole evening for you. Are you being so killed for God's sake first and then for your own sake? And if so, with what sword? Is it with some secret and slaughtering providence of God toward you in your home life, or in your business life, or is it deep down beneath all that and in your heart of hearts which God alone sees? Is it some secret sword of God under which you are fast bleeding down to your grave? Well then attend to this one parting pastoral word. Turn your thoughts every day, Jacob Behmen would say every half-hour, away from the men and the women around you and think you see those men and women above you who through much tribulation are now made for ever perfect. Think you see David and his choirs, and Paul and his readers, and Shepard and his New England hearers. But above all think you see and hear Jesus Christ the Man of Sorrows, and every single sorrow of His for His Father's sake and for your sake. Find the place and read it every day to your own sin-slaughtered heart, how He Himself was brought as a lamb to the slaughter and as a sheep before His shearers was dumb. And, especially, have this concerning Him always ready to hand: Father!

save me from this hour. But, no ; since it was for this cause of Thine that I came to this hour Father ! glorify Thy Name. Then there came a Voice from heaven saying, I have both glorified it, and will glorify it again.

XII

'I KEPT A PRIVATE FAST FOR THE CONQUEST OF MY PRIDE'

IN 1642 they kept real fast days. On occasion they denied themselves meat and drink and sleep and re-creation, and gave themselves up to meditation on divine things, and to self-examination, and to public worship, and to private prayer. And Thomas Shepard was a true seventeenth-century Puritan in the way he laid out his whole life for the salvation of his soul. For these are his very identical words written in a small manuscript book that little did he think would be opened and read with such great honour and such great love in the city of the Scottish Covenants in the year of his risen Lord Nineteen Hundred and Nine. These are some of his then secretly-written but now openly-read words about himself: 'November 10, 1642. —I kept a private fast for light to see the full glory of the Gospel, and for an infused faith, and for a spirit of prayer, and for the conquest of all my remaining pride of heart.' This deep-hearted

and many-sided man had more things than one
in his mind when he set himself to keep his
private fasts.   But he had nothing that was
more in his mind than his own proud and un-
humbled heart.

Now to begin with, you must all know quite
well what pride is and what a proud heart is.
It is pride and it is a proud heart to have high
thoughts about yourselves.   It is to have high
thoughts about your great worth as compared
with the worth of all other men.   It is to have
high thoughts about your rights and about
your titles and about your highly deserved
honours and rewards.   It is to go about carrying your head high and laying all other men's
heads low.   It is to be haughty and scornful and
arrogant and domineering.   It is to speak and
to expect that all other men shall be silent.
It is to be so swollen in your souls that you can
brook no rival near your throne.   In a word it
is to be as like the devil himself as a mortal man
can be.   For a proud heart is understood to have
been that fallen angel's one besetting sin according to the Hebrew prophet's apostrophe directed
down to him which runs thus : 'How art thou
fallen from heaven, O Lucifer, son of the morning !   For thou didst say in thine heart, I will
ascend into the highest heaven.   I will exalt my
throne above all the other stars of God.   I will
be like the Most High Himself.'   And the
greatest, but at the same time the most humble-
minded of all the apostles, warns a young and

a gifted minister to take good heed lest, being lifted up with pride, he fall into the same condemnation with the devil.

I think I will put this lesson in the very forefront of all our lessons this evening : this painful lesson concerning the immense losses that we all suffer because of the pride of our heart.   Our immense losses that is in self-knowledge and in self-improvement.   We are all full of faults that our best friends simply dare not venture to point out to us, such is the pride of our heart.   Our very best friends and our very wisest well-wishers cannot run the risk that is involved in telling us the simple truth about ourselves.   We would so turn upon them if they did.   We would so strike back at them if they did.   We would so remember it against them.   We would never forgive them.   We, all of us, have fatal faults that all men see and speak about behind our back, but our very best friend has not dared as yet to tell us one of our faults to our face.   In all my own acquaintance I only know one man to whom I can be bold to tell to his face all the things that you tell to one another behind his back.   And, would you believe it ? instead of resenting my boldness with him, that saintly man only loves and trusts me all the more. Have you any such saintly man as that in all your circle ?   But far more to the point, are you such a saintly man yourself ?   If not, fast from your pride till you are.

So sadly true is all this that, if you would live

in family love and in domestic peace with a
proud-hearted man, you must never venture to
instruct him in anything, nor to correct him in
anything, nor to cross him in anything, and
especially, you must take good care not to do
anything of that sort in the presence of other
people. One day when old Mr. Shepard was out
visiting his congregation he went on their warm
invitation to take tea with a happy pair he had
married to one another just the week before.
In the exuberance of his honeymoon the gushing
young husband was pouring out all the talk on
all the topics that came up in the conversation.
When at one point his gentle wife with all her
sweetness quietly corrected him in something in
which he was quite wrong. She should not have
done it. For she had no sooner done it, than her
husband turned on her and gave her such a look
and such an answer as made Shepard shiver to
his bones.

As I read the scene in Shepard's diary of
that day I remembered the brave-hearted bride
who said, ' No, sir ! ' when the officiating minister
asked her if she would have this man who stood
beside her to be her husband. ' No, sir ! ' she
said and walked out of the astounded church
and back to her mother's house. She had been
a few minutes too late in arriving at the church
door ; and in the offended pride and the hot
anger of his heart her bridegroom had given her
such a look and had hurled at her such a word
as I shall not here repeat. And thus it was that

with a flash of sure foresight down the coming
years she lifted her head nobly before the over-
awed congregation and said, ' No, sir !' and thus
escaped just in time from a life of cruel bondage
to a man with a proud heart and a bad temper
and a bitter tongue. ' No, sir !' she said, and
went away back to her old home a free woman.
Again I say to you, and Thomas Shepard bids
me say it to you out of his own experience, that
if you would live in domestic peace with most
men you must never know anything better than
they know it, nor must you speak till they have
spoken. And when they have spoken you must
always admire and applaud what they say. As
the apostle also has it—the wife see that she
reverence her husband.

Let us take our next illustration of a proud
heart from public life, but not from the public
life of the present day. In Dr. Newman's
Apologia a story is told by him, and with great
approval, about a certain saint called Alphonso,
who began life at the Italian bar but ended his
life in a Roman monastery. On one occasion in
the pursuit of his professional duties Alphonso
was betrayed into what seemed to many to be
an act of deceit, though as a matter of fact it
was only an intellectual mistake he had made in
getting up his case, and that was the occasion
of his leaving public life and embracing what is
called the ' religious life.' All his friends tried
to quiet and console him by assuring him that
such mistakes were not uncommon even among

the best men at the bar. But so crushed was
the young advocate's proud heart that he would
listen to nothing that any one could say to him.
But with his head sunk on his breast he said,
'Vain world! I know you no more! Courts of
law, never shall you see me again!' And turning
his back on the scene of his humiliation he with-
drew to his own house saying aloud all the way,
'Vain, vain world! I know all your vanity now.'
The people in Rome who settle these things may
canonise that man and call him a saint, and for
my part I hope he was; but that was very far
from being a saintly step that he took. A true
saint would have fasted from his pride, and would
have returned to his post, and would have been
all the more commanding in his eloquence and
all the more successful in his cases that he was
more and more from that day clothed with
modesty and with humility. It was not his
saintliness, as Dr. Newman would have us believe, that turned Alphonso away from the work
of his life; it was his all-consuming self-esteem.
It was his sinful pride and not his saintly
humility that made Alphonso a monk.

> We need not bid, for cloistered cell,
> Our neighbours or our work farewell,
> Nor strive to wind ourselves too high
> For sinful man beneath the sky:
>
> The trivial round, the common task,
> Will furnish all we need to ask,—
> Room to deny ourselves, a road
> To bring us daily nearer God.

But I cannot cast much of a stone at runaway Alphonso. And that because I have sometimes been very near doing the same thing myself. When a Scottish minister makes a great breakdown because of his laziness, or because of his bad temper, or because of his want of common sense, he does not have a monastery into which to make his escape. No. But there are new vacancies announced every day in some one of which he may hope to get a hearing, and perhaps a call, and so be able to flee the scene of his many mistakes and his great humiliations. O no, my brother, do not do it! Remain where you are and face it out. Stand to your post and play the man. Continue to live on in the same manse in which you and your young wife were once so happy. And, God helping you, go out and in among your present people adorning every week-day your Sabbath-day doctrines of repentance and reformation. And your humble-minded retrieval of your past errors, and your universally recognised reformation for the future, will impress and will instruct your people far more than all your early blamelessness of life and devotedness to duty ever did. God saves the meek. I was brought low. He did me help afford.

Among all your public and private fasts for the conquest of your pride, do any of you ever fast from self-excusing, and self-defending, and self-asserting? We have already taken a great lesson from the life of a Roman Catholic saint, let us

humble ourselves to take another lesson from
another such saint, and a far better. 'It is a
mark,' she says, 'of the deepest and the truest
humility to see ourselves blamed and censured
and condemned without a due cause, and still to
be silent under that great wrong. It is a very
noble imitation of our Lord to be so silent. For
myself,' she says, 'I could never make trial of
this so Christian grace in any matter of much
consequence, because I never heard of any one
speaking ill of me that I did not see how far
short he fell of the full truth. For if he was
quite wrong in his present particulars, I had
offended God much more in other matters that
my detractor knew nothing about. And methought God favoured me much in not having
my worst sins proclaimed before all the world.
And thus I am always very glad that my slander-
ers should tell a trifling lie about me rather than
the whole terrible truth.' Now, if any of you
are as much 'trysted with fault-finders' as
Thomas Shepard and Santa Teresa were, you
might try their private fast from self-defending
and from self-excusing and see how it would
turn out.

In the Scriptures and in the best old divinity
all true fasting is always accompanied with much
true prayer. And there is nothing you can do
that is so certain to kill out all the remaining
pride of your heart as true prayer united with
true fasting; true heart-searching, heart-breaking, heart-outpouring prayer. 'When Ouranius

first entered into holy orders he had a great haughtiness in his temper and a great contempt and scorn for all foolish and unreasonable people. But he has prayed away that proud spirit till he has now the greatest patience and tenderness even for the most obstinate sinners. The rudeness or the ill-nature or the evil tongues of any of his people used at first to betray him into retaliation, but now all these things raise no other passion in him than more prayer in their behalf. Thus have his prayers for other men, as well as for himself, altered and amended his whole heart. This secret life of prayer of his enlightens his mind, and softens his heart, and sweetens his temper, and make everything he says and does to be instructive and impressive and amiable and affecting.' And so on to the end of his splendidly-painted portrait. And not Ouranius only. But the same life of true prayer—heart-searching, sin-confessing and intercessory prayer—will soften and will cleanse the rudest and the most ill-natured of men among you. Pray far more, my brethren. And the things you will have to confess about yourselves every day will soon show you that pride was not made for such sinners as you are. Yes, true and unceasing prayer is guaranteed gradually to kill out all your remaining pride. True and unceasing prayer will end in making the proudest man among you as meek as was Moses himself: aye, as meek and as lowly in heart as was Jesus Christ Himself.

That being so, I do not think I can wind up better than with the proud man's prayer. Will you join Jeremy Taylor and me in offering it? Well, it is this: 'Thou, O God, wilt Thou do something for the proudest of men also? Make me humble-minded, and lowly in heart. Take away from me all this spirit of pride and haughtiness and ambition and self-flattery; all this self-confidence, and all this unseemly gaiety of mine. Teach me to love concealment; teach me to love to be little esteemed. Let me be heartily ashamed of all my past sin, and all my present folly. Enable me to bear reproaches evenly, for I have fully deserved them all, and to refuse and to lay down all the honours that are offered me because in reality I have deserved none of them. Also to suffer all reproof thankfully, and then to amend all my faults speedily. Invest my soul with the humble robe of my meek Master and Saviour Jesus Christ. And when I have humbly, patiently, charitably, and diligently served Thee on earth, change my confusion into glory, my folly into perfect knowledge and true wisdom, and all my weaknesses and dishonours into the strength and the beauty of the sons of God. And in the meantime use what means Thou pleasest to conform me more and more to the sweet image of Thy Son. Make me gentle to all men and only severe to myself. Make me willing to sit down in the lowest place, striving to go before my brother in nothing but in doing him and Thee honour and service. Grant me all this, O God, for His sake who humbled Himself to the Cross, and who is now with Thee in my behalf my Example and my Advocate; to whom be all glory, and all praise, and all dominion, for ever and ever. Amen.'

XIII

'THE THOUGHT OF MY FAST-COMING DEATH OFTEN MAKES ME VERY UNHAPPY'

 UST as I was stepping out of the steamboat at the pier of Weggis on the Lake of Lucerne one evening the other week these words shot suddenly into my sin-troubled mind: CHRIST IS THE END OF THE LAW FOR RIGHTEOUSNESS TO EVERY ONE THAT BELIEVETH. And all that night and for several days after I walked about as with wings. I am often like Thomas Shepard in my thoughts about my coming death but all that night I was more than a conqueror. Such a great light shone all that night upon God, and upon His holy law, and upon Christ as the end of God's holy law, and upon myself as a believer, and upon my pardon and my peace and my acceptance in Christ, and upon all that I needed for my life and my death and my abundant entrance into the new heavens and the new earth wherein dwelleth righteousness. Now, why am I not always like that? And why was Thomas

Shepard not always like that? And why are you
not always like that? Will you give me your
best attention for a short discussion of some of
the questions connected with your fast-coming
death and mine?

Well then to begin with, 'it is appointed to
all men once to die,' says the apostle. 'Sentence
of capital punishment has been passed upon every
one of us,' says the stoic. 'Now I saw in my
dream,' says John Bunyan, 'that betwixt them
and the gate there ran a river, but there was no
bridge over the river, and the water of the river
was very deep. At the sight of the river therefore the two pilgrims became much stunned in
their minds. "Is there no other way to the
gate?" they asked the man. And at the answer
they got the two pilgrims, and Christian especially, began to despond in his mind. And though
he looked this way and that he could find no
way whereby to escape that so deep-running
river. And entering he began to sink, till he
cried out to his friend, "I go down into deep
waters, and all His billows and all His waves go
over me."' No; there is no other way but the
way of that river for any one of us.

And then there is nothing else in our future of
which we can be so absolutely sure as that river.
The oldest and the wisest of us are still full of
plans and purposes and hopes and expectations
for this life. But all the time we may never see
so much as one of the things for which we so
much wait and expect. Only there is one thing

we shall all one day see whether we look for it or no. 'Go to, now, all ye that say, To-day or to-morrow we will go into such and such a city and continue there a year, and buy and sell and get gain; whereas ye know not what shall be on the morrow.'

And then there is this also. There are many enterprises in life in which if we fail at our first essay we may hope to succeed at our second. In a battle, in an election for some post, in a school or college examination some of our very best scholars will sometimes come short in their first trial only to attain a brilliant success at their second trial. I often recall my first schoolmaster who was wont to march us little boys round the schoolroom to this sounding couplet:

> If at first you don't succeed,
> Try, try, try again!

And I have lived long enough to prove the wisdom and the truth of those early lines. But all the time there is a limit to the truth and the relevancy of that. For if we do not score a success in our first death we shall have no second chance given us. If we had a second chance of shooting that awful gulf we would practise the terrible leap day and night till we were absolutely sure of securing a foothold on the other side at our second trial. But no! 'It is appointed to all men once to die, and after that the judgment.'

But it is time to take up some of Thomas Shepard's reasons why so many of his best people died so unwillingly and so uncomfortably. And he tells us one outstanding case in his New England congregation as a sample of many more. He was hastily summoned one day to the death-bed of one of his best elders. And he had no sooner entered the sick-room than the dying man cried out: ' Oh, Mr. Shepard, I did not expect this so soon and so suddenly! And I am not at all ready! I feel that I am going fast, but where I am going I know not! I thank you, sir, for all that you have done for me and mine. But God has forsaken me, and I well deserve it. Oh that I had another Sabbath day under you in that dear old church! Oh that I had another communion day, you breaking the bread! Would I not prepare myself for it! But that is all past for me!' Bad as the case looked, Shepard was a skilful physician, and the dying man departed this life that day in evangelical peace, if not in full assurance.

Then there is sometimes this also. The sins of their long past youth come back savagely on some men when they are laid down to die. A long lifetime of repentance and of faith and of prayer and of fruitful service may have come in between their early days and their deathbed, but an old conscience of sin takes no account of all that. A cruel conscience of former sin has no respect for a reformed life, no nor for a penitent deathbed. ' Ah, my friend, my friend! The sorrows of death have compassed me, and the pains of hell have got hold of me! And with

that a great horror of great darkness fell upon
him, so that he could not see before him. Here
also in great measure he lost his senses, so that
he could neither remember nor orderly talk of
any of those sweet refreshments that he had met
with in the way of his pilgrimage. Here also he
was much in the troublesome thoughts of the
sins he had committed both since and before he
began to be a pilgrim. Hopeful therefore had
much ado to keep his brother's head above water.
Yea, he would sometimes be quite gone down,
and then he would rise up again half dead. Ah !
brother, said he, surely if I was right He would
now rise to my help. But it is for my great sins
that He hath brought me into this snare and so
hath left me.'

Another thing ; take care lest you die in your
present sins, our Lord says to us in some of the
most solemn words He has ever spoken. And
that not without good reason. For some of His
not wholly untrue disciples will sometimes be
found dying under the continued dominion of
lifelong sins that make their deathbeds almost as
dark as hell itself. I never forget, but often
make my own, old Bishop Andrewes's confession
that he had been in a great trespass from his
youth up, and was still in that great trespass of
his in his saintly old age. Some of you will be
like him and me. You will know quite well the
names and the places and the occasions of your
deathbed-darkening sins, unless you escape their
dominion in time. For unless you crucify them

more than you have ever yet done, the day is at the door when they will bite like a serpent and sting like an adder.

Yet another thing. You will sometimes find some of God's servants dying most uncomfortably because of something He has laid upon their hands to do for Him and which is not even begun to be done; some public service, some domestic duty, some assistance not given to the Church of Christ, some pension not paid to some of His poor, some bitter dispute to assuage, some reconciliation to seek, some broken friendship with some men to be put into repair, and so on. The truth is, it is a wonder that any man among us ever dies in peace of conscience with so many causes of reproof and remorse crowding round his deathbed. Seeing the negligent and the selfish lives that some of our not wholly ungodly men live, the wonder is that they have so few bands in their death. And it is to be doubted if their freedom from such bands is a very good sign of their case.

And then, as I have said to you a thousand times: Have your best books near your deathbed and well within your reach. Aye, have your best books near you while yet death has not knocked at your door. The last time I saw one of our most godly-minded members in his widowed room, he was sitting with his cup of tea on his lonely table, and with his well-worn Bible lying open between his cup and his plate. Do you know that simple-looking sight made a deep impression upon me. So much so that I could not but tell it at his funeral service. Again, the first pastoral visit I made after I came to St. George's was to an old elder of Dr. Candlish's who was on his deathbed. And I see the thing as if it had been yesterday. There lay open on his pillow—what book do you think? His Bible? No. The *Pilgrim's Progress*? No. The *Saint's Rest*? No. *Rutherford's Letters*? No. I will tell you what it was, for you would never guess. It was the *Westminster Confession of Faith*, and it was open at the great chapter on justification. ' I am dying on that Gospel chapter,' he said. And I had no sooner finished it to him than he fell asleep in Christ his Righteousness. On the other hand, I was at another deathbed the other day, and there was neither a Bible nor any of the above books in all the room. And when I asked for a Bible, one was at last rummaged up at the bottom of a drawer full of family rubbish, cast-off clothes, and such like. Show me your most favourite books and those nearest your table and your bed, and from them I will read your prospects when you come to die. And often read in your Bible. Very few people ever open their Bible unless it is to find the text in church. I never all my life came on a man or a woman with their Bible open on their tea-table but the true saint of whom I have just told you. Not one in a hundred read their Bible to call reading. Even those people who read Bunyan and Baxter and Rutherford very seldom read their Bible to be called reading. And thus it is that few people know where to turn in their Bible when they come to die. Yourselves, for instance. When do you read in your Bible? Where, and how much, and how long at a time? And what are your favourite Scriptures? And what will you ask your minister to read and open up to you when every other book has failed you? Read the best books and only the best. Read like that unbaptized heathen who said that he never read a book but to make himself a better man. Read only the best books, but, as Brea said, Always run your pipe up to the fountain.

But far better than merely reading your Bible will be the constant employment of your evangelised imagination on all you read. As Newman says, think you see the Four Last Things: Death and Judgment and Heaven and Hell, and that by God's blessing will prepare you for dying as nothing else will. Compel yourself sometimes to think you are now in the act of dying. Forefancy your deathbed, as Rutherford counselled one of his correspondents to do, and which he did with such success. Read sometimes the intimation of your death in the paper. Open your eyes in imagination on your bed in hell. Imagine, which you will easily do, that you have sinned away for ever your long lengthened-out day of grace. Or, on the other hand, imagine that where sin abounded grace has much more abounded. Till the first sound after death to

you is the Voice of Christ saying to you, ' Come,
thou blessed of my Father.'   Open your eyes in
heavenly imagination and see Him whom your
soul loveth.   And standing around Him and
waiting for you your father and your mother
and your minister, and with them those great
authors and great preachers to whom you owe
your soul.   Read your Bible and all your best
books in that way, and when you come to die
and to live again you will have your everlasting
reward for your humility, your teachableness,
and your obedience.   But take the best advice
of all.   When in spite of your best books and all
your best preparation your old sins come back
upon your bed as Christian's ghosts and hob-
goblins came back upon him when he was cross-
ing the river : then, instantly, and with all your
might, and with all the lifelong practice of that
you have had, betake yourself to the Blood of
Christ, which is also the Blood of God, as Paul
said it was to the old elders of Ephesus.   Take
it as an English contemporary of our American
author has it : ' When your old sins crowd around
your deathbed and stare you in the face have
instant resort to the blood of atonement.   And
as you lay *aqua fortis* upon letters of ink to eat
them out, so still be dipping the hands of thy
faith in the Blood of Christ.   This do every
moment that is now left thee, and that so awful
handwriting that was recorded against thee,
when it is sought for it shall no longer be found.'
Or as we had it at the beginning of this discourse,

'Christ is the end of the law for righteousness to every one that believeth.' As Rutherford sings it :—

> I stand upon His merit, I know no safer stand,
> Not even where glory dwelleth in Immanuel's Land.

XIV

'MY SINS ARE SOMETIMES CRUCIFIED BUT THEY ARE NEVER IN THIS WORLD MORTIFIED'

RUCIFIXION was an all but universal method of capital punishment among the ancient Egyptians and among the ancient Assyrians and among the ancient Greeks and Romans. So much so that an ancient author tells us how Alexander the Great crucified some two thousand of the captured inhabitants of Tyre in one day. And Josephus, the Jewish historian, tells us that after the fall of Jerusalem the Romans crucified so many of the defenders of that city that the forests of Judea failed at last to supply trees enough for crosses, such was the vengeance and such was the savagery of the Roman commander against the God-forgotten Jews.

When a great malefactor, or the unhappy victim of a commander's vengeance was condemned to be crucified, he was taken by his executioners and was nailed by his hands and

his feet to the cross. And then he was left
hanging on his cross till he died of loss of blood
and of starvation. After which the wild birds
of the air and the wild beasts of the field would
gather around his dead carcase. Now all that
rose most powerfully and most experimentally
before Paul's imagination when he was penning
his Epistle to the Galatians and when he said to
them that all they who are the true followers of
Jesus Christ have so crucified themselves with all
their evil affections and evil works and evil ways.
As also when he was writing to the Romans and
when he said to them, ' Knowing that our old
man is crucified with Christ, that the body of sin
might be destroyed, that henceforth we should
not serve sin.' Now, what exactly would it be
for any of those Galatian or Roman Christians
and for any of ourselves so to crucify any of our
remaining sins ? What exactly does the Apostle
mean us to do when he appeals to us that if we
would indeed be Christ's we must continue every
day and all our life long to crucify our flesh with
its affections and its lusts ?

Well, let us take some of those sins that the
Apostle specially denounces to the cross, and let
us clearly see what it is he would have us do to
those sins of ours. Take hatred, for instance,
that besetting sin of ours which he so often
denounces. Now there are times of temptation
to us all when our hearts are as full as they can
hold of hatred and malice and ill-will against
such and such men. So much so that we could

kill them if it were only safe for us to do so.
Well at that murderous moment we are commanded to arrest and to condemn that wicked
passion and nail it to its cross. As soon as any
hatred to any man stirs in our hearts we are to
denounce it in the name of Christ crucified and
we are to crucify it that moment as upon His
Cross. And then with the nails hammered into
its hands and its feet, and with the sword of God
through its heart, we are to watch it on its cross
till it is stone dead so as never to hate God or
man any more. And so must it be with all our
variance and with all our wrath and with all our
envy, as the Apostle goes on to tell us. And to
all that we make answer, O Holy and Sweet
Spirit of all brotherly love! Come in Thy love
and power and enable us to condemn to the cross
this hell-born spirit of envy and ill-will. Come
and assist us to crucify every hand and every
foot of our so indwelling and so besetting sin!
Arrest every movement of grudging and grieving
in our hearts at our neighbour's good! Cast us
not away in loathing from Thy presence, O God,
and take not Thy Holy Spirit from us!

Vainglory is another sinful affection of ours,
against which the Apostle shows as much bitterness as if it had been his own besetting sin. That
is to say, all our hungering for, and hunting after,
the approval and the applause of men. And those
men among us whose lives are so weakened and
whose hearts are so enslaved by this miserable
mind, they will thank the Apostle for every honest

and noble word of his concerning their special case.   Up! then, all of you who depend for your happiness and for your usefulness on the puffing-up praises of mortal men!   Up and shake off this ignoble weakness of yours.   Up and simply crucify to death your so self-seeking heart.   Nail up your vain mind to the outcast and shameful cross of your Saviour.   Starve your vain heart of its inflating food till it dies of sheer starvation. Refuse to read or to hear any of the sweet things with which you have been wont to feed and indulge its contemptible life.   For, unless you simply crucify your secret love of flattery and adulation, it will come to this that you will not be able to live without your daily dose of it. Your love of flattery and adulation is like your dram-drinking—you must have it administered stronger and stronger, and oftener and oftener, till you die for want of it.   ' If we live in the Spirit, let us walk in the Spirit.   Let us not any more be desirous of vainglory: provoking one another, envying one another.'

But so bent is the great Apostle on our full salvation from all our sins that their mere cruci-fixion does not satisfy him.   Nothing will satisfy him short of their full mortification.   For cruci-fixion after all is only crucifixion.   But morti-fication is more; mortification is death.   Morti-fication is absolute death: it is complete, and final, and everlasting death.   A crucified man may continue to live for hours and even for days after he has been nailed to his cross.   But after he is dead, he is for ever dead. And so is it with a sin. A sin may continue to live, and as a matter of fact it does continue to live for days and weeks and months and years after it has been crucified. But, when once it is dead, it is for ever dead. Nailing a sin to its cross; denying it all its former freedom of action and all its former food and keeping it nailed on its cross, so that it cannot rob or murder any more—that is its crucifixion. But all the time so to crucify a sin is not yet to mortify it, as Paul himself knew to his cost. For, if ever any man's sins were crucified, it was the Apostle's sins. But at the same time if ever any man's sins were still alive and unmortified, to his unspeakable wretchedness, it was Paul's sins. In that great crucifixion chapter of his which in some respects is the greatest chapter the Apostle ever wrote, we see this great distinction fully and clearly taken between the true crucifixion of sin and its full mortification. We see so as never to forget that great distinction in every sigh and sob and agonising cry that rises to heaven out of every verse of the seventh of the Romans. And besides, in that great experimental chapter as in all the Apostle's corresponding chapters, we are taught that while every saint's self-crucifixion is his own immediate and ever-urgent duty, at the same time the full and final mortification of all cruci-fied sin is the proper work of Almighty God alone. And more than that, this great work of Almighty God within us will only be fully

finished when we awake at last in His holy likeness: when, as our hymn has it, 'Time and sin
together cease.' For then and then only shall
we be for ever dead to sin and for ever alive unto
God; like as, and as much as, Jesus Christ Himself. And so shall we be for ever like Him, and
for ever with Him.

Now, from all that, every man here at all in
earnest about his salvation from his sin will see
that he must make up his mind and lay out his
life to crucify all his several sins and to keep
them crucified, till God has time to have them
for ever mortified. For, if a malefactor was once
arrested and was crucified and was kept crucified
till at last he died upon his cross, in that case his
days of robbery and murder were at an end. But
let the watching soldiers fall asleep, or let them
become drunken, and let that crucified criminal's
old companions come and take him down from
his cross, as sometimes happened, and that rescued
malefactor would immediately return to his former
crimes and even worse than before. And so will
it be with those robbers and murderers who are
still alive and unmortified in our own unsanctified
hearts. They may be really and truly crucified
and their days of open and outward transgression
may seem to be at an end. But cease watching
them; cease for so much as a day or an hour from
keeping them crucified, and they will be back
that very hour at all their former evil works.
Yes, communicants, watch well from this com-
munion-day all your to-day crucified sins and

set a special watch over them all after this communion season is over. For those bosom sins
and those so besetting sins of yours that are
to-day nailed to their cross and are silent and
motionless and shamming death, unless you watch
with all your watchfulness they will be down from
their cross and will be back again at all their
evil ways as soon as this crucifixion week is over.
Wherefore watch and pray as never before.

And then, if that is your determined and
sworn resolution to-day, take home with you this
great evangelical comfort upon which Paul also
lived and died. This great evangelical comfort
that all truly crucified sin is already forgiven sin :
it is wholly forgiven even where it is not yet
wholly mortified. Paul's own indwelling sins
were very far from being wholly mortified as yet.
But while that was so he was enabled to say, and
that with the fullest assurance of faith, I thank
God, through Jesus Christ my Lord, that there
is to me now no more condemnation. And not
to me only, but there is no condemnation to any
one who like me walks not after the flesh, but
after the spirit. Come, he says to all his readers
who have a good conscience concerning crucified
sins—come and let us reason together. For who
is he that condemneth ? It is Christ that died,
yea, rather, that is risen again, and who is at the
right hand of God making continual intercession
for all those who are crucified on His cross and
in His strength. Who then shall separate even
the chief of sinners from the love of God ? Shall

tribulation, or distress, or persecution, or famine, or nakedness, or peril, or sword? Or sin? Augustine added to Paul, to which bold addition let this only be added : No sin shall separate us from the love of God, if only it is truly crucified and is kept crucified till God the Holy Ghost has had it for ever mortified. Wherefore comfort your hearts with that apostolical and evangelical comfort, all of you who are the sin-assaulted and sin-tortured children of God. For, if you suffer with Christ crucified now, one day soon you shall also reign with Him. I shall be satisfied, said the psalmist, when I awake with His likeness.

But come for a moment and step softly into Thomas Shepard's sickroom and listen to the last words of that great pilgrim father. 'O my sinful heart!' he is still exclaiming as we enter his room. 'O my often-crucified but never wholly mortified sinfulness! O my life-long damage and my daily shame,' he still cries after his own manner and in his own words that we know so well. 'O my indwelling and so besetting sins,' he exclaims, 'your evil dominion is over now! It is now within an hour or two of my final and everlasting release! For I am authoritatively assured that by to-morrow morning I shall have entered into my eternal rest! And then, O my ransomed soul, one hour in heaven will make me forget all my hell upon earth!' So felt and so spake Thomas Shepard with his last breath in this world. And even so had Paul felt and spoken on the morning of his martyrdom, and thus of

his final mortification from all his exceeding sinfulness. And so shall you and I feel and say
some morning before very long. For:

> Hark the glad sound, the Saviour comes !
>   The Saviour promised long ;
> Let every heart exult with joy,
>   And every voice be song !
>
> He comes the prisoners to relieve,
>   In Satan's bondage held ;
> The gates of brass before Him burst,
>   The iron fetters yield.
>
> He comes ! the broken hearts to bind,
>   The bleeding souls to cure ;
> And with the treasures of His grace
>   To enrich the humble poor.

XV

'I WAS SALTED WITH SUFFERING'

ONE great use of salt is to preserve from putrefaction. And one great use of suffering is the same. But salt is not only necessary for preservation it is absolutely necessary also for our full health and for the full strength and the full stability of our bodily life. And so is suffering absolutely necessary for our spiritual life. Peter has a passage exactly parallel to Shepard's preface where he says with a touch of autobiographic sympathy and authority, 'The God of all grace, who hath called us to His eternal glory by Christ Jesus, after that ye hath suffered awhile, make you perfect, stablish, strengthen, settle you.' That is Peter all over. Peter's life was spent in a perfect bath of suffering; but what of that, he says, if the God of all grace is thereby perfecting me, and stablishing me, and strengthening me, and settling me, as a salt bath strengthens and settles a frail and an infirm man!

But to go further back than Peter, and to

begin at the Beginning: The Wonderful One
Himself humbled Himself to be salted with suffering, like all His brethren. There are many
literal and repeated and mind-amazing Scriptures
for that. Did you ever try to weigh them in
your mind? Try it now: 'The Captain of their
salvation was made perfect by suffering. . . . In
that He hath suffered, He is able to succour them
who suffer . . . And, though He were a Son, yet
learned He obedience by the things that He suffered.' As His servant Thomas Goodwin says,
our Saviour learned to have a 'lady's hand' by
the things that He suffered: a lady's hand in
binding up our broken hearts and in healing all
the diseases thereof.

And now for a lesson or two from all that.
And first, just think, though it is far above all
human thought, yet still continue to think of all
the knowledge, and all the wisdom, and all the
love of God that is involved and that is employed
in selecting and in administering to each several
one of His people the very exact suffering that is
best suited for each individual soul. It is far
and for ever above us. We shall never be able
to think aright of such a divine thing as that.
But let us labour after it and more and more
attempt it. Just think of the wonderful work
that the God of all grace has taken upon His
mind and upon His heart and upon His hands!
Had He no more men to bring home to His
eternal glory than are assembled in this house
this evening—what wisdom and what grace would

be needed to apportion to each one of us just the exact suffering, in kind and in amount, that we shall need to perfect, to stablish, to strengthen, and to settle us! There are no two of us alike in anything; and least of all in our manifold spiritual putrefactions and in our manifold spiritual necessities of all kinds. Think of that, and then multiply this house by the multitude that no man can number, and you will exclaim, O the depth of His wisdom, and O the far greater depth of His grace!

And then amid all that unfathomable ocean of things, your own salvation will largely lie in your watching for and in your marking and in your constant acknowledging of God's special dispensations of sufferings, as of all else, to your own individual selves. 'Thereafter,' says one, 'I was set by Him to learn a new exercise in His school; which was to consider His end and His design in particular providences towards myself. I was led on to study His ends in all my sufferings, temptations, and afflictions. Till I came upon His mind in some otherwise overwhelming dispensations of His toward me. And in this way I came more and more to see that God was all my life following me about with His greatest loving-kindness.' My brethren, if it is so good even to read of such wonderful things as these, what must it be to experience them and to discover them in a man's own lifelong walk with God. It must simply be heaven upon earth.

At the same time that eminent saint confesses

to us that he was sometimes so beset behind and before with suffering that he was tempted to take the rod out of God's hand and thus to counterwork Him. You understand? You are taking the rod out of God's hand as often as you make an attempt to escape away from a painful providence before you have got the full good out of your pain. It is sometimes put in your power to flee from places and from people who are ordained of God to be His rod for your sanctification. And it is a mark of the very greatest grace attainable in this life when you willingly and joyfully abide under His rod till He Himself sees that it is safe for you that He remove it. Will you think about that all you who are great sufferers of His? And will you wisely and dutifully make personal application of that? Now, will you? 'I was sometimes sorely tempted,' says that singularly submissive saint, 'to take His rod out of His hand, and to do all I could to undermine and to counterwork Him, though I knew all the time that He could be doing nothing else with His rod but working out my salvation. Yes: I would go against him and would counterwork Him even when I could not but see that He was all the time perfecting me, and stablishing me, and strengthening me, and settling me.' So froward and so hard to sanctify are His very best saints.

Another most difficult but all-important lesson is to learn how you are to look upon and to treat those people who are God's rod in laying your sufferings upon you. God does not often inflict your sufferings on you immediately, and with His own direct hand, though sometimes He does that also. But for the most part He takes hold of the evil that is in some of your neighbours ; He takes up into His own hand the evil that is in their hearts and in their lives and in their characters, and He makes use of that evil for your suffering and for your sanctification. You will see Him sometimes taking the cruelty, and sometimes the pride, and sometimes the envy, and sometimes the jealousy, and sometimes the malice, and sometimes the ingratitude, and sometimes the coarse-mindedness, and sometimes the hard-heartedness, and sometimes the sheer stupidity of some of your neighbours, and employing all that as His rod to break your hearts and thus in the long run to save your souls. But it will take the greatest grace on your part to see that and to accept that and to continue to submit to that. It will take great spiritual wisdom, and great spiritual insight, and great spiritual humility, and the greatest faith in God to lay yourselves and to leave yourselves under God's hand in all that. When you greatly suffer at the hand of some of your evil neighbours you are tempted to think of them only and to retaliate and strike back at them. You are tempted to think only of the rod and to overlook the Hand that holds the rod. But, taught of God, you must more and more learn to look away from those men who make you so to suffer till you see

Him only who is working out your eternal call-
ing by all your everyday sufferings. I believe that
this is about the last and the best grace attainable by you in this life of suffering and sanctification.

And then out of this so noble and so Christ-
like state of mind this added mind will arise.
Every wound that evil men inflict on you ; every
pang of suffering that makes you swoon with the
pain of it ; you will come that moment in the
twinkling of an eye neither to see nor to hear your
evil neighbour, but God only. You will come
to this that they will scarcely enter your mind
at all, so full will your mind and your heart and
your life be of God and of His salvation. You
will no sooner again suffer, than that moment you
will bow to His wisdom and will rest in His love,
sure as you will be that nothing shall separate
you from the love of God. And as you enter
deeper and deeper every suffering day into God's
deeper and deeper counsels toward you, as your
suffering life goes on, you will come to look with
a certain holy fear and a certain solemn solicitude
and anxiety on those men, good and bad, who are
causing you such suffering and such temptation.
For though their evil is, for a while, God's employed and over-ruled rod for your salvation ; at
the same time, He will one day call them to a
strict account for all their ill-intended share in
your great sufferings. Even when He makes all
their evil to work together for your good, He all
the time keeps a strict account of all such things

and will one day require it of them in His own
time and in His own way. 'So the angel that
communed with me said unto me, Cry thou, saying, Thus saith the Lord of hosts, I am jealous
for Jerusalem and for Zion with a great jealousy.
And I am sore displeased with the heathen that
are at ease. For I was but a little displeased
with Jerusalem, and they helped forward the
affliction. O cruel daughter of Babylon! I was
wroth indeed with my people, and thus I gave
them into thy hand, when thou didst show
them no mercy: upon my people hast thou no
mercy: upon my people hast thou heavily laid
thy yoke.' Instead therefore of striking back at
those who cause you such suffering, leave them
in God's hand to forgive them after He has made
His full use of them. Look on them with a holy
fear and a holy awe, lest the sufferings that will
be your salvation should end in being their condemnation. 'Wherefore, love your enemies,
bless them that curse you, do good to them that
despitefully use you and persecute you.' Yes,
actually and often pray for them before God,
for their time is coming, unless you pray and
they repent. You are salted with such suffering
in order that you may be made thus perfect.
'Be ye therefore perfect, even as your Father
which is in heaven is perfect.'

XVI

'BRING FORTH THE BEST ROBE AND
PUT IT ON HIM'

THERE must surely be some very special suitability in the symbol of a robe since that so beautiful and so impressive symbol is employed so often in the Holy Scriptures. For from the opening chapters of Genesis down to the closing chapters of Revelation this symbol of a garment and a robe comes forward continually. 'And Adam and his wife,' so we read, 'hid themselves from the presence of the Lord God amongst the trees of the garden. And the Lord God called unto Adam and said to him, Where art thou? And Adam said, I heard Thy voice in the garden, and I was afraid, because I was naked, and I hid myself. . . . And unto Adam, and unto his wife, did the Lord God make coats of skins and clothed them.' Now after reading that so suggestive Scripture you will be pleased to know that all our best mystico-evangelical interpreters find in that far-off Scripture the original introduction to all the fully developed

Scriptures of the New Testament, such as the
Romans and the Galatians. Notably so Arch-
bishop Trench has an exquisitely beautiful sermon
in which he makes us see the whole gracious
mystery of the coming gospel of substitution and
imputation already involved and so far revealed
in that early text. And when we come down to
the evangelical prophet we find the Gospel symbol
of a robe both adorning and enriching the whole
of his beautiful book. As for instance this passage : 'We are all as an unclean thing, and all
our righteousnesses are as filthy rags : But I will
rejoice in the Lord, and my soul shall be joyful
in my God. For He hath clothed me with the
garments of salvation, and He hath covered me
with the robe of righteousness, as a bridegroom
decketh himself with ornaments, and as a bride
adorneth herself with her jewels.' And when we
come to Paul, he is by far the greatest and by far
the best of all the apostles to us, because he is so
full of Gospel imputation both in his own personal experience and in his apostolic doctrine.
' Touching the righteousness which is in the law,
blameless. But what things were gain to me,
those I counted loss for Christ. That I may be
found in Him, not having mine own righteousness, which is of the law, but that which is through
the faith of Christ, the righteousness which is of
God by faith.' And so on through all the
Epistles of that great Apostle ; in all of which
the justifying righteousness of Jesus Christ is
written as with a sunbeam. And so is it in its

own dramatic and symbolical way in the whole
of the Book of Revelation. As thus for one
example : ' I counsel thee to buy of me gold tried
in the fire, that thou mayest be rich ; and white
raiment that thou mayest be clothed, and that
the shame of thy nakedness do not appear ; and
anoint thine eyes with eye-salve, that thou mayest
see.' And so on, to the end of that apocalyptical
and heavenly book.

Out of their own bitter experience both Adam
and Eve and Isaiah all foretell us what our bitter
experience also is sure to be. Adam our fallen
father speaks to us from among the trees of the
garden and says to us : ' My confusion is continually before me, and the shame of my face hath
covered me. Mine iniquity hath taken hold upon
me, so that I am not able to look up !' And
from beside him the mother of all living sobs out
this self-accusation to all her offspring : ' Who
can bring a clean thing out of an unclean ? Not
one. How then can any man be justified before
God ? or how can he be clean that is born of a
woman ?' While Isaiah prophesies out of the
temple to all our preachers especially and says to
them : ' Woe is me ! For I am undone ! For I
am a man of unclean lips, and I dwell in the
midst of a people of unclean lips. For we are all
as an unclean thing, and all our righteousnesses
are as filthy rags.' And startling and stumbling
to many unspiritual men as these strong words of
Isaiah are, they have all been subscribed to by all
God's best servants down to our own day. ' Rags '

is the prophet's strong word; while 'dung' is the apostle's still stronger word. And the penitent readers of the *Holy War* will remember Mr. Weteyes who always saw so much impurity in his own tears, and such great stains at the bottom of his best prayers. And in his *Private Thoughts* we find the saintly Bishop Beveridge saying: 'I cannot pray but I sin. I cannot preach a sermon, or hear a sermon preached, but I sin. I cannot receive the sacrament but I sin. Nay, I cannot so much as confess my sins but my very confessions are still so many aggravations of my confessed sins. So much so, that my repentance needs to be repented of; my tears need washing; and the very washing of my tears needs still to be washed over again in the blood of my Redeemer.'

Yes; but after reading and hearing all that we still feel sure that there never can by any possibility have been 'rags' like our righteousnesses in all the world. Such a ragged obedience of God's holy law, such a ragged repentance, such a ragged faith, such ragged communicating, such ragged preaching, and such ragged praying is ours. We feel certain that neither Beveridge, nor Bunyan, nor Paul, nor Isaiah could come near us in the raggedness of our righteousnesses. Only, Blessed be their God who so accepted them in all their rags and wretchedness; and who said over them: 'Bring forth the best robe and put it upon them!' And He will still more exalt and magnify His saving grace in saying the same thing this day concerning us. Yes, concerning us the raggedest and the least deserving of all His servants.

Now the communion-morning pulpit is surely the very last place in the world in which to give vent to a controversial temper. But all the same, I must be permitted in this connection to say this in the interests of truth. For the life of me I cannot conceive how any Christian man can take this ' best robe' to be in any sense whatever his own righteousness. Great names: yes, it saddens me to say it, some of the greatest names, could be quoted in support of that absolutely impossible interpretation. But for myself, were all the interpreters that ever wrote, and all the preachers that ever stood in a pulpit, to take that side, I would be compelled to stand alone on the other side. For I am as sure as I am of my own existence, aye far more sure, that my best right-eousness can never, in whole, or in part, in any sense, or in any measure, justify me. My own righteousness can never, in life, or in death, or on my resurrection day, or on my judgment day, afford me one single inch of a footing on which I can stand before God, or even before my own conscience. But I thank God that I am not alone in my absolute despair of myself and in my interpretation of the text. For if I may put it in this way, I have Adam, and Eve, and Abel, and Abraham, and Moses, and David, and Isaiah, and Micah, and Paul, and a whole Pauline succession down to this day standing beside me and I

beside them.   An evangelical and an apostolical
succession down to Chalmers, and M'Cheyne, and
Spurgeon, and Maclaren, and all subscribing with
their tears and their blood to the all-justifying
and the all-covering and the all-adorning righteousness of their Redeemer-surety Jesus Christ.
' A review of my life,' writes John Foster—the
famous essayist, ' back through all these years
brings bitter reflections to me of the wretched
deficiences neglects and vanities '—he should just
have said ' filthy rags '—' of a life that ought to
have been wholly devoted to God.   But, since
that has not been so, my daily and almost hourly
prayer is this—God be merciful to me a sinner !
I do think,' he adds, ' that if there be any one
thing that I am fully clear of—it is self-righteousness.'   Intending communicants, is that your mind
about yourselves ?   Because, if so, this morning's
text will be spoken from heaven over you as you
approach the table.   ' Bring forth,' it will be said,
' the best robe, and put it on him.'

No.   This is no robe of ours that we can ever
bring with us, or could ever weave for ourselves
on any loom of our righteousness to all eternity.
This is the ' best robe ' in all the rich wardrobe
of heaven itself.   Even had Adam and Eve stood
to the day of their death or of their translation,
and had all their righteous seed gone on working
out their own righteousness to the day of judgment: CHRIST is better: Christ the Son of God
is far far away better.   As Paul so like himself
has it: for his part he counted all his best blame-

lessness to be but the most ignominous thing he could think of, that he might be found in Christ. And many of you have by heart the masterpiece and immortal passage that is not unworthy to stand even beside the third of the Philippians. That glorious passage can never be more opportune than it is at this moment. Listen to it: 'Christ hath merited righteousness for as many as are found in Him. In Him God findeth us, if we be faithful: for by our faith we are incorporated into Christ. Then, although in ourselves we be altogether sinful and unrighteous, yet even the man which in himself is impious, full of iniquity, full of sin: him being found in Christ through faith, and having his sin in hatred through repentance; him God beholdeth with a gracious eye, putteth away his sin by not imputing it, taketh quite away the punishment due thereunto, by pardoning it; and accepteth him in Jesus Christ, as perfectly righteous, as if he had fulfilled all that is commanded him in the law. Shall I say more perfectly righteous than if he had fulfilled the whole law? I must take heed what I say: but the Apostle saith, God made Him who knew no sin to be sin for us: that we might be made the righteousness of God in Him. Such, then, we are in the sight of God the Father, as is the very Son of God Himself. Let it be counted folly, or frenzy, or fury, or whatsoever. It is our wisdom and our comfort: we care for no knowledge in the world but this, that man hath sinned, and God hath suffered: that God

hath made Himself the sin of men, and that
sinful men are made the righteousness of God.'
For my part, let it be counted folly, or frenzy,
or fury, or whatsoever, I think I would rather
have written those heavenly lines than all the
rest of the English language taken together.
Do you feel with me in that this morning? I
am sure many of you do. Many of you must do.

Dr. Pusey, the best Hebrew scholar of the last
generation in the English Church, holds firmly
that in that great justification-passage which we
read together this morning, where it is written
that Joshua the high priest stood clothed with
filthy garments, till the command came forth
that he was to receive change of raiment: that
great Hebraist holds that both the Hebrew verb
and the New Testament doctrine agree in this
that Joshua *always* stood clothed with his own
filthy garments, and with those of the people of
Israel, and as such was *always* receiving change
of raiment. I cannot speak with such authority
on matters of Old Testament grammar and exe-
gesis, but I am quite sure that the thing is true
both of New Testament doctrine and New Testament experience. Paul puts it once for all when
he says that ' God always justifies the ungodly.'
And Hooker but expatiates on Paul when he says
(I will give you what he says again): ' Then,
although in ourselves we be altogether sinful and
unrighteous, yet even the man which in himself
is impious, full of iniquity, full of sin: him being
found in Christ through faith, and having his

sin in hatred through repentance: him God beholdeth with a gracious eye, putteth away his
sin by not imputing it, taketh quite away the
punishment due thereto by pardoning it: and
accepteth him in Jesus Christ as perfectly righteous': as Paul has it, 'accepted in the Beloved.'
To gather it all up in the ever-blessed words of
the text, we are *always* returning home from the
far country, and we are *always* saying, 'Father,
I have again sinned.' And our Father is *always*
saying over us, 'Bring forth the best robe and
put it on him.'

Now, communicants, young and old, are you
like that? Do you do that? Have you humbled yourselves so as to submit to Gospel imputation always and without ceasing? 'I am
always sinning,' said Luther, 'and I am always
reading the Epistle to the Romans.' 'I come
back as a prodigal son every half-hour,' said
Luther's greatest disciple. And one who is not
always counted among Luther's disciples was
wont to say every morning when he put off the
garments of the past night, 'I will put on His
righteousness and it will clothe me; it will be to
me for a robe and for a diadem.' Be like them,
my brethren. Be sure to be like them. Be like
them if you would live in liberty of conscience
and in peace with God and in assured preparation for death and judgment. Every morning
you rise put on again the best robe. And every
returning night lie down again in it. Go out to
your day's work always wearing it. Make it your

morning coat and your evening dress. Be married
in it, if you would be married in the Lord ; and
make it your winding-sheet, if you would die in
the Lord.   Die in it and awake in it and go up
to judgment in it.   Stand at the right hand of
the great white throne in it, and enter heaven
shining like the sun in it. 'What are these which
are arrayed in white robes, and whence came they ?
These are they which came out of great tribulation, and have washed their robes and made them
white in the blood of the Lamb.'

O great Absolver !   Grant my soul may wear
The lowliest garb of penitence and prayer,
Till, in the Father's courts, my glorious dress
Shall be the garment of Thy Righteousness.

And then—

When I stand before the throne
Dressed in beauty not my own :
When I see Thee as Thou art,
Love Thee with unsinning heart :
   Then, Lord, shall I fully know,
   Not till then, how much I owe.

Meantime :

Here is my robe, my refuge, and my peace,
Thy blood, Thy righteousness, O Lord ! my God !

XVII

'FIAT EXPERIMENTUM IN CORPORE VILI'

'FIAT experimentum in corpore vili' is an old Latin proverb to the effect that the Divine Operator takes only the vilest and the most worthless of men to make His greatest experiments upon them. Now our students of surgery sit apart in their seats and watch with more or less sympathy while the most classical experiments are being made on the poor patients who are strapped down on the operator's table. But it is only when a student has been overtaken himself with the same deadly disease and is himself strapped down on the same table, it is only then that he fully understands how the diseased part feels, and how the knife feels, and how his new health feels when it begins to come back to him. Now if you have never as yet been laid down on the divine table, nor have come under the divine knife, then sit still and study at a safe distance what all those subjects of His have to undergo at His hands on whom the God of their health makes His most famous experiments and works His most famous cures. At your present stage you can have no idea of the numbers of men, first and last, who have laid themselves down under the knife of the Great Operator, and all saying with the prophet and the pilgrim father, 'From the sole of the foot even to the head.' And saying with the Stoic Emperor also, 'From scalp to sole one slough and crust of sin.' Some of the names of those many sufferers must come to your mind at this moment. But—is your own name among them? That is the one question in this whole world for you and for me. Because there is another world just at the door where the inhabitant shall not say I am sick; a world such that all they who dwell therein shall be forgiven their iniquity.

But to begin with, what correctly and exactly is here meant by 'the sole of the foot,' with all its wounds and bruises and putrefying sores? Well, surely this. As our outward man stands upon his foot, and upon the sole of his foot, so does our inward man stand first upon his mind, upon his understanding, and upon his power of thought. 'From his deepest foundations upwards,' says Pascal, 'man is made to think. His whole manhood, his whole duty to God and to man, is simply to think about God and about man and about himself as he ought to think. That is the whole obligation and merit and dignity of man.' And again, the same deepest of thinkers says: 'How great and how grand is

the mind of man! And how vile and how hateful
is the mind of man in its corruptions and in its
pollutions!' 'Think much,' says Teresa also to
her thinking readers: 'meditate much on the
terrible hurt that your mind has received from
the fall.' And surely no man who has a mind
within him, and who attends to what goes on
within him, can but think continually, and with
the most solemnising thoughts, on the great
disaster that has somehow befallen his mind.
For what a doleful fountain of selfish thoughts is
the mind of every man, and of foolish thoughts,
and of disordered thoughts, and of mistimed and
misplaced thoughts, and of brutish thoughts,
and sometimes of absolutely diabolical thoughts!
Who among us could endure for a single day
that all his secret thoughts should be known to
any of his fellow men? Rather would we cry
with the lost at the last day: Rocks! fall on us,
and hide us and these our evil thoughts from the
face of God and man! Now the one point in all
this world for a truly wise man is to find out
how his so wounded and so bruised mind is to be
closed and bound up and mollified with ointment.
Well, surely, the first step to a perfect cure is to
see and to admit that all this that the prophet
says about himself and about all Israel is true of
ourselves and of our own mind and the thoughts
of our own mind. And then we must be humbled
to the dust every day we live because of our condition simply as thinking men. We must be
like Agur, that wise man of the East, of whom

it is recorded that he said to himself every day and every night after every day: ' Thou, Agur, hast again thought evil thoughts, thou hast again spoken evil words, and therefore thou hast again to lay thy hand upon thy mouth.' Yes, wise Agur, thou hast divine wisdom with thee. For silence, absolute silence from all self-esteem and all self-defence is the proper part of all such sinful men as we are. A silence only broken by constant confession and by constant prayer. Humility of mind, and a daily and hourly endeavour to fill his mind with the wisest and the holiest thoughts: that is the true part, and the becoming part, for every man who by the enlightenment of God has discovered somewhat of the disorders, and the corruptions, and the pollutions of his own mind. ' His sole delight,' says the first of the Psalms, ' is in the law of the Lord, and in His law doth he meditate day and night.' And working in that way at the healing of his mind, ' he shall more and more become like a tree planted by the rivers of water, that bringeth forth his thoughts, and his words, and his deeds in due season. His leaf also shall not wither, and whatsoever he doeth shall prosper.'

> Sight, riches, healing of the mind,
> O Lamb of God, I come !

Now we are all following that with our understanding. But it is just here that our will comes in either to make what we have just heard our salvation or our condemnation. One of us will hear what has been said and will assent to the truth of it and will with his whole will determine to do it and will be blessed in the deed. Another of us will hear all that has been said about the state of his mind, and, though he cannot deny the truth of it, he will turn away from the truth and will start objections to what has been said or to the way it has been said, in order to justify himself in not doing the truth he has heard. In other words, his will is all wrong. His understanding is not wholly right, but his will is far worse than his understanding. A man's will is himself; it is his very self. And by his will he is able willingly and resolutely to turn away from the truth. A man's will is as it were the helm of his whole life. And when the helm is moved the wrong way, the vessel is steered straight to destruction. 'Our wills are ours,' sings Tennyson, 'to make them Thine.' Christ's will was His to make it His Father's. And He made His own will His Father's will when at that tremendous crisis-hour for Himself and for us He took the cup from His Father's hand and said, Not My will but Thine be done! His will was a submissive will and a holy will and a sonship will long before that, and all along; but it became a still more submissive and a still more holy and a still more sonship will in Gethsemane and on Calvary. And we all have our Gethsemanes and our Calvarys offered to us and placed right on our path, in order that we may say what He said and may do what He did. In our Lord's words—

that we may take up His Cross upon our own will every day and then follow Him to where He now is.

> I worship Thee, sweet Will of God !
>   And all Thy ways adore,
> And every day I live I seem
>   To love Thee more and more.
>
> Thou wert the end, the blessed rule
>   Of Jesus' toils and tears ;
> Thou wert the passion of His heart
>   Those three and thirty years.
>
> He always wins who sides with God,
>   To Him no chance is lost ;
> God's will is sweetest to him when
>   It triumphs at his cost.
>
> Ill that He blesses is our good,
>   And unblest good is ill ;
> And all is right that seems most wrong,
>   If it be His sweet Will !

But neither the mind nor the will nor anything else that is within us is so wounded and so bruised and so putrefied as is our sinful conscience. Our sinful conscience makes our country desolate like Isaiah's country ; and our city to be burned with fire like Jerusalem ; it makes our city to be almost like Sodom to us and almost like unto Gomorrah. Now I will speak to the man with the most torn and tortured conscience in this house of God this night, and he will hear me. What was it, sir, that so tore your conscience to such wounds and bruises and putrefying sores as these ? Come, and let us reason together—what was it ? What was your very worst and most conscience-exasperating sin ? Was it your breaking some one's heart ; some one whose name has for long years been written in letters of hell-fire on your forehead ? Was it ruining some one's life ? Was it beggaring some man that trusted you ? Was it bringing your father's and your mother's grey hairs with sorrow to the grave ? Or was it some still more scarlet and crimson sin than all these ? For the sinfulness of some men's sins is simply unspeakable and unthinkable to any one but themselves and their victims. Well, sir, there is only one ointment in all the world that will close and bind up and mollify such a conscience as yours. But blessed be God there *is* such an ointment. And Paul entrusted the name of that ointment to the elders of Ephesus ; and perhaps he did so because there may have been one man like you in that session of saints who needed that ointment every day he lived. And the name of that conscience-healing ointment is nothing less than the BLOOD OF GOD.

> Not all the blood of beasts,
>   On Jewish altars slain,
> Could give the guilty conscience peace,
>   Or wash away the stain.
>
> Thy work alone, O Christ !
>   Can ease this load of sin ;
> Thy blood alone, O Lamb of God,
>   Can give me peace within.
>
> His blood can make the vilest clean ;
>   His blood availed for me.

So sang Charles Wesley.

On one occasion a professor of surgery was taking a company of students round the beds of an incurable hospital when he came to a couch on which a man lay who was full of wounds and bruises and putrefying sores. Referring to some last and despairing operation that was to be performed on that living corpse the professor said to his students, 'Fiat experimentum in corpore vili!' 'Too true, gentlemen,' said the dying man, 'too true. But, pro hoc corpore vili, Jesus Christus mortuus est.'. That is to say: 'Too true, gentlemen, but Jesus Christ died for this vile and worthless body and soul of mine.' The dying outcast was a graduate and a prodigal son of his Alma Mater the University of Cambridge. 'Pro hoc corpore vili,' he said, in a Latin that startled the students.

So much as to the mind and the will and the conscience. As to the imagination I shall let the prophet Ezekiel speak: 'Furthermore, He said to me, Son of man, seest thou what they do? And when I looked, behold a hole in a secret wall. And He said to me, Go in, and see, and tell abroad, what they do in the chambers of their imagery. So I went in, and I saw'—you all know what he saw. It is as our own Carlyle has it: 'his imagination is either the hell-gate or the heaven-gate of every man's heart. And then, in that man whose imagination has been the gate of hell, his whole head is sick and his whole heart faint. From the sole of his foot even unto his head there is no soundness in him, but wounds

and bruises and putrefying sores. But even to
that most miserable of men the heaven-gate of
his soul is not yet closed for ever. And if he will
henceforth use his *mind* aright, and his *will,* and
his *conscience,* and his *imagination*—behold, a
ladder set up on the earth, and the angels of God
ascending and descending upon it. And Jacob
awaked out of his sleep, and he said, Surely, the
Lord is in this place! This is none other but the
house of God, and this is the gate of heaven.

Speaking about Santa Teresa Pascal says that
what so commended that wonderful woman to
the men of her day and to all men ever since was
her splendid mind ; whereas what so commended
her to God was her so utterly broken heart. And
how broken her broken heart was you all remember who have ever read about her deathbed.
She saw everything put into its proper place, and
every one answering to their proper order, after
which she attended to the divine offices of the
day, and then went back to her bed and summoned her daughters around her. ' My children,'
she said, ' you must pardon me much. Do not
imitate me. Do not live as I have lived. For I
have been the greatest sinner in all Spain. I have
not kept the laws that I laid down for others.'
And then she turned her face to the wall and
said ; ' O Lord, the hour I have so much longed
for has surely come at last. It is surely time
that I was taken out of this banishment. The
sacrifices of God are a broken spirit ; a broken
and a contrite heart Thou wilt not despise.

Create in me a clean heart, O God. A broken and a contrite heart' was her continual cry till she died with these words on her lips, 'A broken and a contrite heart Thou wilt not despise.' My brethren, it is a heart like David's heart and Teresa's heart and your heart that God binds up with His own hands: pouring into its wounds His best wine and His best oil. He closes all such wounds with His own hands; binding them up and mollifying them with that one ointment, the name of which you know.

Well then, before you go down to your own house—How is all this with you? What is your wound? What is your bruise? What is your putrefying sore? Is it a secret tumour of swelling pride? Is it a secret abscess of brutish impurity? Is it a secret and an ever-gnawing envy? Or is it some malformation of the heart that you have inherited from those who went before you? Well all that taken together will not be able to kill you. All that taken together will only make your cure all the more classical and all the more unparalleled in the 'Transactions,' so to call them, of the Church of Christ. Meantime take these first principles of the Divine Hospital home with you. Give your mind and your will and your conscience and your imagination and your heart to these few first principles and make constant application of them to your own case. (1) It is God's love that so cuts you to the quick. (2) There is to be no myrrh allowed nor chloroform nor any kind of mental or moral insensibility. (3) No pain no cure; little pain little cure; great pain great cure; lifelong pain here everlasting life without any more pain in that land where God Himself shall wipe away all tears from His patients' eyes. (4) All His divine operations are performed in secret. (5) All His divine operations are performed free and for nothing: for His Hospital is fully endowed for the service of the poor. And (6) A perfect and an everlasting cure is absolutely guaranteed: absolutely guaranteed against all possible relapse.

Fiat! Fiat experimentum in corpore vili!

XVIII

'PECTUS FACIT THEOLOGUM'

PECTUS facit theologum—that is to say it is the heart that makes the theologian. Not the head. Not talent. Not learning. Not power of speaking. Not power of writing. Other men may be made without much heart. Men of scholarship may be made without much heart. Men of science may be made without much heart but not men of religion. Not men of science even, according to Dr. Newman's eloquent argument entitled ' The Philosophical Temper first enjoined in the Gospel.' But, be that as it may, it is indisputable that it is the heart that makes the true theologian. Take Paul, the first and the best of theologians, take Athanasius, the father of Christology, take Augustine, take Luther, take Hooker, take Chalmers, and it was their heart above all things else that made them all what they were. In elucidation then, and in illustration of this subject, let us take the text and run it through some of the various departments of true theology and of true religion and we shall soon see how true the text holds everywhere that it is the heart that makes the true theologian.

But to begin with, what is a true theologian? and how does his heart come to make him what he is? Well, a theologian, a true theologian, is just that man whose whole discourse is of God. God is the greatest and the best of subjects on which the mind and the heart of any man can discourse. For God is love. And the seat and the throne of love in God and in man is the divine and the human heart. And consequently the more love any man has in his heart the better able he will be to know God and to discourse concerning God. A blind man will far sooner discourse aright concerning colour, and a deaf man concerning sound, and a dead man concerning life, than any man who is not a partaker of the Divine Nature will discourse aright concerning God and concerning the love of God. I need not labour that matter a moment more. For it is as clear as day that love to God and man will alone make any man a true theologian. As our proverb has it—Pectus facit theologum.

In the second place, it is the heart that makes the true exegete; that is to say the true expositor, the true annotator, and the true commentator on the word of God. A Hebrew scholar can read the Hebrew Old Testament, and a Greek scholar can read the Greek New Testament, and an English scholar can read the whole English Bible. But the best reader of both the Old and the New Testament is the man who brings his whole heart

to bear upon the book of God. The eye sees
that only which it brings the power to see. And
the mind reads only what it brings the power to
read. And then the heart both sees and reads
and feels what it alone has the power to see and
to read and feel. And that is the love of God as
that love is written, as with a sunbeam, on every
page of the Divine Book. God had His own
Book written for us out of his own heart, and
the more of God's heart any man has in himself,
the better able will that man be to read for himself, and to draw out for other men, the whole
mind and the whole heart of God from the Book
of God. As face answers to face in water, so
does the heart of God answer to the heart of
man ; and, again, so does the heart of man answer
to the heart of God in the sacred writings. In
other words, it is the heart that makes the truest
and everyway the best expositor of the word of
God and the best annotator thereupon.

And not the true theologian and the true
exegete only, but it is the heart that makes the
true apologist also. Under this head I shall stand
aside and I shall let the prince of apologists
speak to you. And I shall let him speak first to
you on the true proof of the fall upon which
everything afterwards turns. ' The undeniable
proof of the fall,' he argues, ' is that man is a
poor, miserable, weak, vain, distressed, corrupt,
depraved, selfish, self - tormenting, perishing
creature. And, in addition, that this present
world is a sad mixture of false goods and real

evils. A scene of all sorts of trials, vexations, and miseries ; and all arising from the frame and the nature and the conditions both of man and the world. This is the full and infallible proof of that awful fall of man which is not to be learned from any history however ancient and however sacred, but which shows itself everywhere, and every day, with such clearness as we see the sun. My first attempt, therefore, upon any man, to convince him of the fall, as the background of the redemption, should be an attempt to do that for him which affliction, and disappointment, and sickness, and pain, and the approach of death, have a natural power to do ; that is to convince him of the vanity, and the poverty, and the misery of his condition and his life in this world. For, as this is the true proof of the fallen state of man, so man can only be convinced of it by having all this proof of it brought home to himself.' So much for the fall. As to its worst consequence—indwelling sin— listen to the same master in Israel. 'Who has not, at one time or other, felt a sourness, and a wrath, and a selfishness, and an envy, and a pride rising up within him wholly without his consent, and casting a blackness over all his thoughts ? Sufficient indications, surely, to every man that there is a dark guest within him, which will, on occasion, show itself, and which may be his torment to all eternity. And it was with His eye on this hidden hell within us, that our blessed Lord said when on earth, and says now to every

M

one of us: "Come unto Me, all ye that labour and are heavy laden, and I will give you rest."' And again, and from the same powerful pen: 'All outward fires, chains, torments, slaveries, poverties, are but so many passing shadows of the tormenting slavery of a sinful soul, left and given up to its own selfishness and envy and pride and anger. And in spite of all denials, and all alleviations of these things, one or other of these elements of hell will sometimes awaken so violently as to become absolutely intolerable, and to give a man a true and sure foretaste of the nature of hell in the soul of a lost sinner.' And that same so powerful pen goes on with its apology in this evangelical way: 'All the mercy of God, to such as we are, is to be found in Jesus Christ. Jesus Christ alone can save us from our sins. He alone has power to heal all our diseases, and to restore us to our original righteousness. And with Him to help us it matters not what our diseases are: deadness of heart, blindness of mind, covetousness, wrath, pride, ambition, lust, and such like; our remedy is always one and the same; and it is always at hand, and it is always sure and certain and infallible. Seven devils are as easily cast out by Jesus Christ as one. And if you ask where Christ is to be found, I will in apology answer, in your own heart and nowhere else. But you will say to me that it is just your own heart that keeps you such a stranger to Christ, and keeps Him such a stranger to you, because your heart is a very den of devils. Now to that

I answer that your finding this to be the real
state of your heart is already the finding of
Christ in your heart. For nothing else, and no
one else but Christ, can make manifest to you the
sin and misery that is in you. And the Christ
who discovers sin is the very same Christ who
takes all sin away. Be you sure, that as soon as
your sin and your misery make your heart absolutely unbearable to yourself, *that* is Christ already
in you of a truth. For Christ first comes to your
heart as the Discoverer and Reprover of your sin.
Acknowledge then His presence, and His power,
and His grace, in making you to know the plague
of your own heart; and then He that wounded
you will heal you; and He who showed you the
den of devils that is within you, He will not leave
you till He has made your heart into a holy
temple, for the indwelling of the Father, and the
Son, and the Holy Ghost.' And in another
place the same unanswerable reasoner proceeds :
' The whole of the Christian religion stands upon
these two pillars, namely, the greatness of our
fall and the greatness of our redemption. In
the full and true knowledge of these foundation
truths lie all the reasons of a deep humility, a
deep penitence, and a daily self-denial. As also
all the motives and incitements to an immediate
and a total conversion from sin to God. Nothing
can truly awaken a sinner but a true experience
of the depth and the power of his indwelling sin.
When he sees and feels that he lies chained deep
into the very jaws of death and hell ; and when,

along with that, he is assured that the free grace
of God has provided a Remedy equal to his
disease : when a lost man once truly feels and
knows these two foundation truths — then no
other proofs of the fall and the restoration are
needed by that man.   Now we believe, said the
men of Samaria to the woman at the well, not
because of thy saying, for we have heard Him
ourselves and know that this is indeed the Christ,
the Saviour of the world.'

And before I close the prince of apologists, I
cannot withhold from you this apology of his for
prayer. ' He who has learned to pray has learned
the greatest secret of a holy and happy life.
Which way soever else we let loose our hearts,
they will return to us empty and weary.   Time,
and the experience of life, will convince the
blindest of us that happiness is no more to be
found in the things of this world than it is to
be dug out of the bowels of the earth.   But when
the motions of our hearts are motions of piety,
tending to God, in constant acts of devotion and
love and desire, then we have found rest for our
souls.   Then it is that we have conquered the
misery of our nature.   Then it is that we have
found a good suited to, and equal to, all our
wants : a constant source of comfort and refreshment, that will fill us with true peace here and
eternal happiness hereafter.   For he that lives in
a devotional spirit, he whose heart is always full
of God, he lives at the very top of human happiness.' Paley is very instructive and very interesting

and he is all that in classical English. And Butler is always very profound and very solemnising. But the apology, of which these passages are specimens, is conclusive, and silencing, and unanswerable, and satisfying to every capable mind and honest heart.

Now, to tell you the truth, I am afraid to take speech in hand again myself after such a defender of the truth as that. But I have one or two things in my mind that I would like to say to you and to myself before I close. And one of them is this—that it is the heart that makes the true preacher as well as the true apologist. For one thing his heart supplies the true preacher with fresh and powerful and home-coming texts continually. A class-fellow of mine complained to me after he was a year settled that he had totally run out of texts for his sermons. I remember how I told him that if he had a heart like mine that would never happen to him. No. No preacher, old nor young, will ever run out of great texts who takes his sinful heart with him to his family worship and to his pastoral work and to all his more retired reading of his Bible. The sinful-hearted preacher who does that will not get peace to die, so many great texts will throng around his deathbed, demanding that he shall arise and shake himself and come back to his pulpit to handle them before his people as he only can. 'I commend you to your own sanctification,' said Samuel Rutherford to a dried-up young preacher. And the same advice followed out every day and every week will continually dis-

cover texts that neither the preacher nor his
hearers ever heard of before. His daily crosses, his
daily heart-breaks, his daily humiliations, his daily
wounds, and bruises, and putrefying sores, are all
guaranteed to supply him with fresh and sufficient
texts if he lived to the age of Methuselah. He will
soon exhaust ' Euroclydon ' and ' the times when
the Gospels were writ.' But he will never exhaust
the Psalms, and the Gospels, and the Epistles, and
his own heart. No, never! And then when his
heart is in his texts and in his sermons :—

> Lo ! this man's brow, like to a title-leaf,
> Foretells the nature of a tragic volume.
> He trembles, and the whiteness in his cheek,
> Is apter than his tongue to tell his errand.

Tragic or triumphant, no hearer will fall asleep
under such a preacher as that. The preacher,
that is, with the sinfullest of hearts himself.

I have not time to tell you how the heart
makes the pastor as well as the preacher. Nor
have I time to treat of the Church leader and
the Church historian. But I cannot let you go
till I have tried to show you how the heart makes
the hearer as well as the preacher. It was his heart
that made one man a stony-ground hearer when
our Lord was preaching. And it was his heart
that made another man a thorny-ground hearer.
And it was his heart that made another man a
good-ground hearer. And it was their hearts
that made His hearers say what they said after
another sermon of His. ' I have bought a piece
of ground,' said one, ' and my whole heart is in

my new farm.' And another, 'I have bought
five yoke of oxen, and I must away at once to
see how they plough.' And another, and with a
shining face, 'I have married a wife, and I do
not need to come.' Unblest oxen! And ill-
matched and unhappy wife! Only, from all that,
we who are preachers need not be too much cast
down. For even when the Son of God Himself
was the preacher, it was His hearers' hearts that
decided their destiny. You who are hearers
might do this, on occasion. You might try the
device that helped to make Thomas Goodwin
such a good preacher. It is told of the Atlas of
Independency that he always took a turn up and
down in his past life before he ventured again
into the pulpit. And I am convinced that the
thing that so helped to make him a good preacher
would help to make you a good hearer. A turn
up and down in your past life on your way to
church would be a good preparation for sitting
down in your pew. And then such a heart in
the preacher met halfway with such a heart in
the hearer, all that could not fail to end in the
best results for us both. Now in one word if it
is the heart that makes the hearer as well as the
preacher, I do not need to detain you to tell you
how and when and from Whom you can at any
time you like get a true hearer's heart:

> A heart in every thought renewed,
>   And full of love divine,
> Perfect, and right, and true, and good,
>   A copy, Lord, of Thine!

XIX

' I ABHOR MYSELF '

JOB loved himself and defended himself and exalted himself till the time
came to him when he began to see
and to understand something of
GOD.   But when he once saw some-
thing of GOD, ever after that Job simply abhorred
himself and repented every day in dust and ashes.
Now why was that?   Why did a dawning sight
of GOD produce such a deep change and such a
lasting change in God's servant?   It was because
he now began to see something of God's great
goodness, and something of the beauty of God's
great holiness, and something of His essential
and everlasting love, and something of His
boundless grace and truth.   And in all that
God's servant saw what he ought himself to have
been all along but was so far from being even in
his old age.   When, having once seen something
of God, Job turned to look at himself—from the
sole of his foot even to his head, he saw himself
to be full of wounds and bruises and putrefying
sores.   And all his self-righteousness, about which

at one time he had been so eloquent, was all
turned now to so many filthy rags, and to that
dunghill on which he sat clothed in sackcloth
and ashes ever after.

And as a matter of fact all God's greatest
servants in all lands and in all languages have
been like God's great servant Job in all that.
And in no land and in no language more than
in our own. I do not need to speak to you
of David, and of Asaph, and of Heman, and of
Isaiah, and of Jonah, and of Joshua, and of
Peter, and of Paul. You all have by heart all
that those great servants of God saw and felt
and said concerning themselves in every psalm
and prayer and sermon of theirs, as soon as they
saw something of God and something of themselves. I will come down at once to our own land
and to our own Church and to our own day and
I will tell you about some men who were more or
less like ourselves. John Calvin is not much
given to autobiography, unless it is in his golden
commentary on the Psalms. But in one place
and with all his directness and with all his plain-
spokenness and with all his laconicness, Calvin
says that ever since he has seen God he has seen
that his own self-love has made him to be a
malicious man to other men. Now, if you know
what it is to be a malicious man to other men
yourself, you will see in that one word how that
great servant of God has made the most damning
of admissions about himself. For to be a malicious man to other men is neither more nor less

than to be, in that, a child of the devil. 'Myself am hell!' said the devil himself in an outburst of autobiography when he looked up into God and then looked down into himself. But all this time the point is not about Job, nor about John Calvin, nor about the devil, but the whole point is about you and me. Well, has our self-love made you and me to be malicious to other men? The most malicious of us are not malicious at all times and in all circumstances and to all men. O no! The most malicious of us are sometimes, and to some men, as soft as butter and as sweet as honey. For let a man be fortunate enough to be on our side; let him pass over into our party; let him become profitable to us; let him be clever enough to see through us, and let him be mean enough to flatter us to the top of our appetite for praise, and we will love that man as our own soul. But let that man cease to be on our side; let him leave our party; let him become disgusted with our fawning hunger for his flattery; let him in any way go against us; and then let us look up into God and down into our own hearts! Did you ever do that? I have, and I know what I am saying. Paul also did that; and, as often as he did it, he again uttered the heartbroken cry that you all know so well. Poor Paul! And poor Job! And poor John Calvin! It was his own malicious heart that made Paul a Calvinist. And it was his own malicious heart that made Calvin a second Paul. But from their example and their experience we

are happy to learn that neither great saintliness
nor great service is denied to the truly penitent,
however malicious they may have found themselves out to be. And, therefore, neither you nor
I need be wholly without hope.

Take next the great Atlas of Independency
who was Calvinior Calvino in everything but in
the immaterial matter of Church government.
All true Independents have that master in their
Israel by heart, especially in what he says about
himself when once he has seen something of his
God and Saviour, and then in that piercing light
has seen something of himself. 'Myself,' he says,
' is the most disingenuous and abominable principle that ever was.' And where Paul says that
by nature we all live in malice and in envy,
hateful and hating one another, our Atlas adds
to that this terrible comment of his — *homo
homini lupus.* And again in this fierce self-
condemning passage : 'Self-love is the very devil
himself in us. It is the prince of the devils in us.
It is the deepest root and the ultimate bottom of
all our sin and all our iniquity. And to dethrone
this house-devil from any man's inmost heart will
take all God's almighty power to do it, and with
all His almighty power He will not be able to do
it wholly in this world.' 'Yes,' he exclaims
against himself again, ' the predominant principle in us all is that we love ourselves more than
we love our neighbour, or even our Maker
and our Redeemer; and in this abominable
self-love lies the bottom of all our original sin, if

you study original sin a thousand years.' And
again : 'There is one great lust, and it is the
greatest of all the rest.   When holiness held the
heart of man the love of God subjected the love
of a man's self unto God.   But take this love of
God away and then self-love is the next heir to
the throne, and it steppeth up immediately into
the royal seat.'   And again, in his agony over
himself, the same truly Pauline man demands of
all his hearers: 'Do you know or can you
imagine what multitudinous shapes this Proteus,
this monster of self-love, will be turned into on
occasions -and in circumstances ?   Unto what
depths of wickedness it will sometimes be
broached forth, and into what infinite varieties of
operations ?   Look about you throughout the
whole world, read the histories of all ages, but
above all,' he demands, 'read your own heart.'
All rightly read Independents will tell you where
I have read all that and more than I have told
you.   It is all to be read with a broken heart
under Goodwin's index on 'Self,' and ' Self-love,'
and 'Self-seeking.'   I am not an Independent in
Church government because I was born a Pres-
byterian.   But I have been a lifelong student
of the Atlas of that sister Church.   And what I
owe him in the knowledge of my Saviour and of
myself I may have an opportunity of telling him
in that land where self-love in him and in me
shall have been transformed into love to God and
to our neighbour for everlasting.

All this time Bishop Butler has been standing

within arm's length of me. And I do not for a
moment forget what that great moralist has said
in some of his stateliest pages. 'Your self-love,'
he tries to calm and to comfort me by saying:
'All your self-love is originally and naturally
good. Yourself, and your love of yourself, is
coincident with the principle of virtue. And,
indeed, is part of the very idea of virtue. And
it is a proper and an indispensable motive for
you and for all men.' But the deepest of English
bishops in saying all that is away back at the crea-
tion-scheme and Eden-state of our human nature.
He has not yet come down to our poor human
nature in its present state of overthrow and dis-
memberment and dislocation and self-destruction.
But when Butler does condescend to come close
to the mind and heart of man as all men now are,
even he becomes as outspoken and as full of pathos
and passion as if he were an evangelical Puritan.

But let us be open-minded and truly catholic
in all our studies, and above all in our study of
God and of ourselves. And that we may be so
this evening let us pass on to take two or three
great Roman Catholics who are all at one with
Job and with Paul and with Calvin and with all
the Puritans when they come to see first God
and then themselves. Did you ever come across
the saintly Abbé Grou? If so you will remember
this passage on the matter in hand. 'Myself is
my worst enemy,' says the Abbé. That is to say,
we may have enemies who would hurt us even
fatally if they only could. But the Abbé's point

is that they cannot. And he is entirely right all through his home-coming argument. For no enemy of mine has ever hurt me as I have hurt myself. I know that there are enemies of mine who would poison my life of all its peace and of all its usefulness if they only could. But they cannot. At the same time let them not be too much cast down on that account. For there is one who can do and who is daily doing what they cannot do. A man's foes to be called foes are in his own house; that is to say they are in his own heart. ' Know thou,' says another Catholic, ' that the love of thyself doth do thee far more hurt than anything else in the whole world.' Yes, Thomas, but we shall never know that by merely reading the *Imitation*. We must read ourselves. We must study, as we study nothing else, our own self-rent and self-distorted hearts. And then Pascal, that so powerful and so far-shining genius in the things of the soul : ' Of all hateful things,' says Pascal, ' myself is the most hateful to me.' We begin life by hating the men and the things that hurt us. We hate the men who oppose us and resist us and hinder us : the men who speak and write and act against us. We bitterly hate all the men who humble us and despise us and trample upon us and in any way ill-use us. But afterwards we come round to forgive, and not seldom to justify those men that we at one time so hated. For we come to see what at one time we could not have believed, that all our hurt, to be called hurt, has come to

us from ourselves. And thus we are left with no
one to hate, to be called hating, but ourselves.

And then an Atlas of Episcopacy has a series
of dialogues on this same subject which are far
more interesting and far more valuable and far
more pertinent to me to read than all the
dialogues of Plato himself. You must not be
too much offended at the strength of his language. For *indignatio facit versus.* I condense
and water down several terrible passages into one
page. 'Pray, sir,' said Academicus, 'tell me
more plainly just what this self of ours actually
is.' 'Self,' replied Theophilus, 'is hell, it is the
devil, it is darkness, it is pain, and it is all dis-
quiet. It is antichrist. It is the scarlet whore,
it is the fiery dragon, it is the old serpent of the
Revelation.' 'You rather terrify me than instruct me,' said Academicus. 'It is indeed a
thing to terrify all men,' returned Theophilus.
'For it contains everything that a man has to
dread in this world and in the next. Because,
there is no hell here or hereafter ; no devil outside yourself ; no furious beast, nor fiery dragon,
apart from yourself that can do you any hurt.
You are your own hell, you are your own devil,
you are your own dragon that lives in your own
heart's blood. Die to yourself ; and all your
enemies on earth and in hell will be for ever overcome.' 'But,' said Theogenes a third party who
stood by, 'I fain would understand what it is
that makes myself to be so full of sin and misery.'
'Sir,' said Theophilus, 'it is your covetousness,

and it is your envy, and it is your pride, and it is your wrath and your ill-will. These are the five elements of hell in your heart. As long as a sinner lives among the vanities of this world, his wicked heart may be in a tolerable state. But when death has put an end to all his earthly blinds and cheats, then that soul which is not washed in the blood of the Lamb, and is not filled with His Holy Spirit, that soul will find itself gnashed and devoured by its own cruel and remorseful teeth. It will find itself shut up for ever in its own unsatiable, unchangeable, and self-tormenting covetousness, and envy, and pride, and wrath.' 'God bless you! Theophilus,' said Theogenes. 'For I shall never forget what you have said to me to-night about myself!'

One midnight well on toward the end of his life Thomas Shepard was found lying on his face in his study in a swoon of sweat and tears, and with a copy of the *New England Gazette* crushed together in his lockfast hands. The reason of all that was afterwards discovered to be this. Mr. T. H., Thomas Shepard's bosom friend, was wont to have a sermon of his printed in the *Gazette* time about with a sermon of Shepard's. And both the manager of the journal and all its readers were well known to Shepard to put his friend's sermons far above his for their eloquence and for their English. It is not told how Mr. T. H. took that praise of himself and that depreciation of his friend. But Shepard

made no secret to God and to his own soul how
he took it. For the copy of the paper that
Shepard held crushed in his hands that midnight
contained a specially beautiful sermon of Mr.
T. H.'s. And as Shepard tried first not to see
that sermon, and then turned in prayer to try
to read it and could not, he quite lost all power
over himself and actually fell on his face on the
floor as if his New England study had been the
Garden of Gethsemane. Now unless you have
fallen on your face in that same way and from
that same cause, or from some similar cause, I
do not want to hear your judgment on Job, or
on John Calvin, or on Thomas Goodwin, or on
Bishop Butler, or on Abbé Grou, or on Blaise
Pascal, or on William Law, or on Thomas
Shepard. Your day for passing a right judgment
on all such men and all such matters is coming,
so I both labour and hope and pray. Hold your
peace then on this whole subject till that pro-
strating day comes; that day of days to you
when, like all those great men, you shall see yourself to be the most to be abhorred, the most
malicious, the most wolf-like, the most inwardly
rent and distorted, the most hateful and the most
hating, the most self-tormenting, and the most
Shepard-like sinner on this side hell. And, when
that all-revealing day comes, I for one will submit
to your judgment, first on yourself, and then on all
other men, and all other matters, both sacred and
secular. Meantime do your best to sing and
in tune with all those men the Forty-ninth

Paraphrase from the fifth verse which runs
thus :—

> Love suffers long : love envies not :
>   But love is ever kind :
> She never boasteth of herself,
>   Nor proudly lifts the mind.

And so on for five golden verses.

XX

'MY MIND IS A BUCKET WITHOUT A BOTTOM'

'MY mind is a bucket without a bottom,' said the self-examining and plain-spoken and homely-spoken founder of Harvard. Now Sir James Murray tells us that after all his researches the true etymology of the name is wholly uncertain to him. But the meaning of the name is quite clear. A bucket is a wooden vessel in which water is drawn up out of a well. It is a round wooden pail with an arched handle and with waterproof sides and a waterproof bottom. We do not need to go to the great Oxford Dictionary to tell us what a bucket is. Every child knows quite well what its mother's bucket is. But we do need a rare man; we need a self-observing and an original and a bold and a plain-spoken and an idiomatic man to tell us that all our minds, of which we are all so proud, are like so many wooden buckets and all without bottoms. And then we all need to humble ourselves to admit the truth of that and straightway to set

ourselves to reform our ways of going to church
and of hearing and remembering and putting to
practice the things that we hear in church.

Now when we look well at the text and when
we take the text and in the light of it look well
at ourselves we are all compelled to confess that
our minds also are like Thomas Shepard's mind.
For a mind without spiritual understanding, what
is it but a bucket without a bottom? If you
were to go to the well at your door with a bucket
without a bottom in your hand, you might go on
letting that bucket down and down and down
into that well for a lifetime, but you would take
no water home with you all your days from that
well. Now that is the exact case of multitudes
of people who come to church twice every Lord's
Day. They have plenty of mind and plenty of
understanding in their minds for other days, but
not for the Lord's Day. Their buckets have no
bottom on the Lord's Day for the water of life.
It was the very same sad case with multitudes of
our Lord's own hearers. They came and they
sat till He was done with His sermon and they
came back again next Sabbath and sat till He
was done when they rose up and went away as
they came. Till at last, absolutely wearied and
worn out with such hearers, He put them into
those terrible parables that are preserved to us in
the thirteenth of Matthew. In which parables
He told them that all the time He was preaching He saw the wicked one stealing up to the
seat where they were sitting and catching away

the good seed as fast as He could sow it. As
Thomas Shepard has it, the devil himself came
and knocked the bottom out of those hearers'
minds. And still Sabbath after Sabbath they
brought their bottomless buckets to our Lord's
well till the good angels wept over them and till
the angels of the wicked one laughed at them
and the whole of the bottomless pit resounded
with their laughter every Sabbath day just as
it resounds still. Paul had the same experience
with his hearers also; especially with some women
among them. Till he turned on them one day
and told them that they were ' ever learning, but
were never coming an inch nearer the knowledge
of the truth.' And till in an Epistle full of his
defeated experiences as a preacher he warns all
young preachers not to be deceived by the mere
attendance at church of such unfruitful hearers.
Shall I say it? Yes! I will take boldness to
say it! In my own small and obscure way I have
had my own experiences as a preacher. There
are men and women in this house to whom I
have done my best to preach both faith and duty
for thirty years and they are not one whit better
than when I began. There are people here, and
not wholly ungodly people either, who, Sabbath
after Sabbath, and year after year, resist all the
appeals that are made to them to mend their
ways. I have laid out every art of instruction
and persuasion and appeal upon them that I
could command. I have pointed out their besetting sin to them as plain as words could speak it.

In my defeat and in my despair I have almost called out their very names from the pulpit if so be I might save them from the sins and the faults that everybody sees and laments in them; everybody but themselves. But to no effect. For there they are back at the well again to-night and with their old buckets without a bottom with them. Yes! certainly! I am speaking to you and not to your neighbour!

So much for a mind without true understanding. We come next to a conscience without conviction or contrition. Now, if you hear God's holy law preached every returning Lord's Day, if you hear evangelical obedience preached every returning Lord's Day, and if you go home wiping your mouth and saying that you have done no evil that you need to repent of, what is that but to take your bucket to the well and to go home Sabbath after Sabbath without taking home a single drop of the water of life? To keep his conscience in a state of constant conviction and contrition, the greatest of the Puritan preachers of the seventeenth century was wont every Sabbath morning ' to take a turn up and down in his past life.' And with that to take a plunge down into his heart and into his life for the past week. And that spiritual and evangelical practice of his resulted in making him the most commanding of preachers in the most commanding school of preachers the Church of Christ has ever seen. Now be you like that commanding preacher. Never you come up to church, neither morning nor evening, without a renewed contrition of heart. And you will never return home without having your contrition of heart intensified and spiritualised and evangelised. And then this house of God will be to you a weekly well of God's best salvation. And every Sabbath night after you go home God's elect angels will camp around your house and they will accompany you and will protect you amid all the trials and temptations of the intervening week. Such rewards does God bestow on every man who has a conscience full of conviction and contrition, a conscience full of inward and spiritual tears for all past sin and for all present sinfulness.

Then again what is it to bring up a will with the power of decision in it to God's house and to go home again without a single decision or holy resolution taken in it; what is that but to come up and go home carrying another bucket without a bottom? Now to be plain with you and to go no further back than last Sabbath morning. Did you form a good decision and a good resolution here last Sabbath morning? and have you carried out that good resolution this morning and this evening? I do not know, I have no idea. But there is One who knows and you will have to render an account to Him of what you have heard last Sabbath and then of what you have done this Sabbath. I have not time to tell you the pertinent story of Penitens that busy notable tradesman and very prosperous in his dealings but who died in the thirty-fifth year of his age. If you

have the conscience-searching book at home read
his eloquent history to yourself to-night. And
you will come on this at the end of it : 'Penitens
was here, going on both about his making and his
spending of money in the past, but had his mouth
stopped by a convulsion, which never suffered him
to speak any more. He lay convulsed about
twelve hours, and then gave up the ghost.'

Then again, what is a heart without holy affection but a bucket made of the finest wood but
all the time without a bottom? The best of
hearts are full of cracks and leaks through which
the water of life continually runs out and is lost.
A hopelessly broken bucket lets all the water run
out. But strange to say a hopelessly broken
heart is the very opposite of that. A hopelessly
broken and a never-to-be-healed heart that is the
one heart that carries home the richest supplies
of the water of life where an unbroken heart lets
all that water run out. And then there are all
stages and all degrees of broken hearts. There
are hearts so broken that they feel themselves to
be without one drop of holy love to God, or to
the Son of God, or to the Spirit of God. And
there are other broken hearts that begin to feel
as if they were at last beginning to love and to
obey their Heavenly Father somewhat, and His
Heavenly Son, and His Heavenly Spirit. And
everything they hear in God's house turns to an
increase of holy affections in their good and
honest hearts. O, sirs ! it is a fine thing, I assure
you, for a preacher to have such hearers ! To

have hearers with such minds and such under-
standings and such consciences and such resolu-
tions and such hearts! Something comes to
such a preacher's knowledge during the week that
makes his heart to swell with the assurance that
God is beginning at last to own his preaching.
He hears, all unknown to the doer of it, of some
secret act of a most noble generosity. Or he
meets one of his people in the street whose face
is still shining with the grace and the truth of
last Sabbath. It was such hearers as that who
supplied our Lord with His happy parable of the
good and honest ground. And it was such hearers
and such readers as that who gave the Apostle
the call and the opportunity for those noble bene-
dictions and doxologies with which he begins and
ends his great Epistles. Such as this to the
thoughtful and liberal and magnanimous Philippians, this: 'Not that I desire a gift from you;
but I do desire fruit that may abound to
your account.' It was because the elders and the
deacons and the people of Philippi had a generous
heart above all the other Churches of that day;
it was because of that that the whole Church of
Christ, down to our own day, has in her New
Testament the exquisite and priceless Epistle to
the Philippians.

And then what is a memory carried to church
every Sabbath day without a word remembered
on the Monday; what is that empty memory
but another bucket without a bottom? I will
wager there are a thousand of such persons

in this house this evening. I will wager that
there are not ten persons present who will of
their own accord remember to-morrow morning or once all the coming week either the
text or any lesson of this morning or of this
evening. At the same time I do believe, for I
have the evidence and the proof of it, that a
spiritual mind and a spiritual memory for spiritual
things is on the increase among us. And now,
in connection with our memories for good things,
take this ' use,' as our old preacher calls it, out
of this head. 'There is many a child in New
England,' he says, ' who immediately forgets
all his father's exhortations and all his family
prayers. But wait till many years after when
his father shall be no more ; and when some
sore trial comes to that son, perhaps some similar
family trial ; and then both memory and conscience will awaken after many years and his
father will have joy in heaven for all his sorrow
on earth. One word spoken at family worship
will sometimes awaken twenty years after when
God's time comes to break that man's heart and
to make him remember the great sorrow he must
have been to his father and his mother.' Such is
one of the ' uses ' that this great preacher takes
out of his own awakened memory as often as he
goes back to his father's house and to his father's
godly walk and conversation away back in old
England.

And now to sum up all that in two lessons.
And the first and the most urgent lesson out of

all that is not so much for you as for those who
preach to you. And that lesson for them is this.
Let all preachers who stand in a New Testament
pulpit take good care to dig their pulpit wells
deep down where the living water runs not on
the surface. And let them keep the people's
ways to those deep wells both open and inviting.
Let it never be said of any of your preachers that
the wells, which their fathers digged so deep, their
sons, like the Philistines of old, stopped them
running and filled them with earth. And, especially, let it never be said in divine condemnation
of this pulpit that it is a well without water and
a cloud without rain.

And now all you who are truly convinced that
up till to-night not your mind only but your
whole soul has been nothing better than a bucket
without a bottom, so far as your salvation is
concerned, what are you to do with the state of
things? What but go to the Heavenly Cooper,
so to call Him, who has shown you to-night your
fatal need of His divine help? And He who
made your mind and your conscience and your will
and your heart and your memory at first, and
made them all in His own image, He not only
makes it at first, but He repairs and restores and
enlarges and enriches His own workmanship.
Take then 'all that is within you' back to Him
and He will repair it all and will restore it all
and will perfect it all. Go and tell Him that you
have destroyed yourself, body and soul, and He
will both redeem and restore you. Be you sure

He will.   Resolve where you sit that you will
go to Him for His help.   Resolve to do it to-
night against your proud heart, and against your
stubborn will.   Waken up your mind and consider well your absolutely hopeless case without
His help.   Let Him never be able to say any
more against you that though He gave you a
mind to consider your ways you never did it.
And so doing, so considering your ways this will
be this night's song over you in heaven : in that
heaven where there is no night; ' consideration,'
it will be sung there concerning you :

> Consideration like an angel came
> And whipped the offending Adam out of him.

XXI

'YOU ASK ME WHAT CURED ME OF BEING AN INFIDEL'

ACCORDING to the etymology of his name an infidel is a man who does not believe in God nor in Jesus Christ whom God hath sent.   An infidel is an odious name in your ears I know, but I am not to employ that name in any odious sense to-night nor am I to speak to-night about any odious man.   I know that there are infidels who are far better men than I am.   Indeed, if they were worse men than they are, I would have far more hope than I have of their speedy and entire conversion to faith in God and in their Redeemer.   At the same time, while I am not here to cast odium on any unbelieving man, I hold most firmly that every unbelieving man is in a most odious condition of mind and heart and life.   And I feel sure the day is fast coming when all our infidels will see and will confess and will flee from the unspeakably odious and impossible position that they have taken up toward God and toward His divine Son, Jesus

Christ. 'Wherefore, God hath highly exalted Him; and hath given Him a name which is above every name; that at the name of Jesus every knee should bow, of things in heaven, and things in earth, and things under the earth; and that every tongue should confess that Jesus Christ is Lord, to the glory of God the Father.'

'You ask me what cured me of being an infidel,' writes a great believer and a great preacher. And I will give you his answer to that in his own ancient and identical words. 'Nov. 14th, 1641. I felt overnight much darkness and unbelief. And next morning I saw this mistake that I was making. This mistake, that I believed what I did believe because I saw it to be agreeable to my limited reason; and so I made my limited reason to be my last resolution of all my doubts. And I began to think how it should be otherwise. So I saw that I was to receive the things that God spake in their agreement with reason indeed; but I was not to make this the last resolution of my doubts, though always one resolution. But, then, when I had seen things to be agreeable to reason, yet I was to look upon God's testimony of them in Holy Scripture as the last and the chief light and ground of my settlement. Not to believe that such and such things are true because I think I see them at present to be true; but to believe that God sees things more clearly than I see. For if I believe anything to be true because I see it to be true; much more because God sees it to be true, Who sees it better than I do, and Whose word stakes me down and confirms me in the truth of what I there read.'

And again : ' I did groan under the burden of infidel thoughts, looking up and sighing to the Lord that, if He really existed, as His works and His word did declare Him to exist, He would be pleased to reveal Himself to me by His own beams, and would thus infallibly persuade my heart of His divine existence. Which if He would do, I should account it His greatest mercy to me. And thus it was that after many distressses of mind, such as almost drove me to be mine own executioner, He came between the bridge and the water, and so manifested Himself that I came to see a glory, and a majesty, and a mystery, and a depth in Holy Scripture, which, all taken together, fully persuaded me ; a persuasion that is not wholly lost to this day. So much so, that when infidel thoughts come and knock at my door, I send them away with this answer : Why should I question that truth which I have both seen and known in better days ? ' And again, May 29th of next year : ' I saw with a great persuasion that Jesus Christ really IS, and really LIVES, and really quickens with His own life all those for whom He died. I saw that God DID LIVE, because He spake to me and quickened me, and did work a divine work in me. He was then the living God to me when I heard His voice and felt His hand ; and to want that persuasion and assurance and experience was to be estranged from all life and all peace and all strength in my soul.'

So far deeply experienced Shepard. But to fortify him in his answer to his correspondent and to enlarge and enrich his answer let us go on to put the same question to some other *ductores dubitantium* and to record their answers. And to give Pascal his well-deserved pre-eminence. ' The Gospel to me,' says that towering spiritual genius, ' is simply irresistible. Being the man I am ; being full of lust, and pride, and envy, and malice, and hatred, and falsehood, and all accumulated and exasperated misery, to me the Gospel of the grace of God, and the redemption of Christ, and the regeneration and sanctification of the Holy Ghost, that Gospel is to me simply irresistible. And I cannot understand why it is not equally irresistible to every mortal man born of woman.' Let Pascal be read continually by all those men who have mind enough, and heart enough, and sin and misery enough, to understand that masterly man of French letters and of experimental religion.

One who is, to my mind, the greatest of our Scottish experimental divines—and that is saying much—writing on the same subject of unbelief, has this prayer among his private papers : ' O Lord, if Thou indeed be the Lord, then Thou art almighty, and almighty, surely, to save me. Wilt Thou then condescend to convince me of the reality of Thy divine existence ? Wilt Thou give me some sure proof, and this very night, to convince me that there is a God, and that Thou art He, and that all that which Thy Word says about Thee is absolutely true? O Lord, be not too much offended at this my peremptoriness, for I can bear my unbelief about Thee no longer. Determine Thou Thy way Thyself; only, in Thy mercy, hear my prayer. O, give me a sign, and to-night, in my soul that Thou art and that Thou art the Hearer of prayer.' Could you have believed it, my brethren, that such a great saint as that could be assaulted when so far on in the divine life with atheistical and unbelieving thoughts such as these? But at this point and in this connection, some class-member present will remember Bishop Butler's appropriate passage which runs thus : ' The chief temptations of the generality of men are the ordinary motives to injustice or to sensual sin. But there are other men who are without this shallowness of soul ; men of a deeper sense as to invisible and eternal things. Now, these rare persons have their temptations set them in the high region of faith, and in the deep region of doubt.' The profound bishop means that while their appetites and their tempers are the great temptations of most men, the grand problems of natural and revealed and experimental religion are the trials and the triumphs of other men ; other men such as Shepard, and Pascal, and Brea, and Bunyan, yes and Bunyan. For you will remember that Bunyan's pilgrim—who, all the time, is Bunyan himself—was neither assaulted nor was even

o

approached by Atheist at the beginning of his journey. That enemy of God and man did his best to ruin Bunyan's soul when he was almost within sight of the celestial city.

To pass by many names of great interest and of great experience and of great power and of great authority, and to come to a name that combines all these elements as no other name has combined them in our day. We find the author of the *Grammar of Assent*, and the *Sermons* and the *Apologia*, and the *Letter to the Duke of Norfolk*, in all these publications and indeed in all that he has published, always and everywhere confessing that it is his conscience which keeps him absolutely and completely cured of all atheism and all infidelity. Were this the time and the place the whole hour could be filled up with his all-commanding proofs of the existence of God, and of God's personal government of all men; all-commanding proofs drawn from the divine nature and the divine judgments of conscience; and all that set forth in a language stately and noble and irresistible almost as the voice of conscience itself. Amid all his changes of Churches and creeds the one thing that cured Dr. Newman of all atheism and all unbelief and kept him all his days near the cross and near the mercy-seat was the overpowering voice of his Maker and Redeemer and Judge speaking to him in his conscience and in his imagination and in his heart; but in his conscience most of all. So that if you had asked him what it was that cured

him and kept him from being an infidel he would
have answered you that it was his conscience;
the all-commanding and the all-overpowering
voice of God speaking to him in his conscience.

But to come home to ourselves. Do you ask
us in this house to-night who are evangelical believers what it was that so cured us of all possibility of our ever being infidels. If you seriously
and teachably ask us that, then I will frankly
and fully tell you. And first; this has been our
frequent and it is still our ever-increasing experience, that the very things which seem to
have made some other men infidels, and even
atheists, these very same things have ended in
making us more resolute and more absolute believers. The greatest sorrows of our lives, the
sorest crosses of our lives, the complete shipwreck
of all our hopes and expectations in our lives, the
great errors, transgressions, and even the all-
desolating sins of our lives, the dark providences
of God, and the hitherto unanswered prayers of
our lives, bad men and bad causes flourishing
like the green bay tree, and good men and good
causes defeated to death; these things, and
things like these, of which this present life of
ours is full, have overthrown the faith of many
men till they have given themselves up to nothing
short of blank atheism. 'My evidencies and my
certainties,' wrote Halyburton, 'were not answerable to the weight I was compelled to lay upon
them.' But by the grace of God to that great
man of God, that faith which is always the gift

of God came and rescued Halyburton from all his unbeliefs and uncertainties and transformed him into one of the noblest believers, both intellectually and spiritually, that ever lived the life of faith in old evangelical Scotland. And the same triumphant faith has been given of God to some of ourselves till we are able to say with Paul himself that neither death, nor life, nor things present, nor things to come, shall ever separate us from our faith in Christ and from our love to God. And to say with Shepard : *Nil tam certum quam quod de dubio certum*, that is to say, in his own free translation, ' Happy is the man all whose doubtings end in establishments.' ' But,' he adds, ' when men settle in scepticism as the last issue of all the debates of their minds, and all the tossings of their hearts, it had been better for such men that they had never been born.'

Then again what Atheist in the *Pilgrim's Progress* calls ' the tediousness ' of the pilgrimage, that has had a great hand in making some half-in-earnest men doubters and sceptics, if not actual scoffers like Atheist. But the very tediousness of the spiritual life ; the very slowness standstillness and even the backslidingness of their sanctification, all that only shuts up some other men the more to what remains of their pilgrimage toward holiness of heart and toward everlasting life. When in their agony they are tempted to say : Doth God know my sufferings of heart, and is there such knowledge with the

Most High? then they recollect themselves and
find the place where this is written, 'Why sayest
thou that thy way is hid from the Lord, and thy
judgment is passed over from thy God. Hast
thou not known, hast thou not heard, that there
is no searching of His understanding? Yes;
the very tediousness, and slowness, and perplexity,
and danger of the Christian life, only make the
true people of God to say the more to whom can
we go? and to whom can we look? and to whom
can we cry? but unto Thee, O my God and
Saviour!

Then again do you ask us what it is that has
cured us of a cold and a shallow and a superficial
faith and has made us evangelical and spiritual
and New Testament believers? What could it
be but our increasing experience of the depth
and the strength and the malignity of our indwelling sin? The sinfulness of our sins, the
corruption of our hearts, and our divinely im-
planted hunger for holiness—all that has made
us to be apostolical and evangelical and spiritual
believers. Our unspeakable sinfulness of heart has
completely cured us of all merely surface sense of
spiritual experience and Gospel holiness and has
shut us up to a life of evangelical and experimental faith in Jesus Christ, in His work, and in
His word, and in His Spirit for our salvation.

To sum up our answer in one word as to what
it is that is curing us ourselves of all our infidelity.
Well in one word it is just our faith. Faith, and
every day more faith, is our divinely-appointed

way of cure. Come and join us then and practise faith with us at all divine times and in all divine things. Practise a great faith in God every hour you live; and in His Son your Saviour, and in His Holy Spirit your sanctifier and your comforter. And above all your books keep reading your Bible; really reading it; secretly and regularly reading it. For your Bible is God's own Book which He has had written out for all true believers and has put into your hand. And His divine Book has His divine seal set upon it so that it will make all its readers true believers; that is to say all who give God's own Book its proper opportunity. Just sit down to it and see. For your Bible is guaranteed of God to make the most doubting of you assured and strong believers. And the most fainting and staggering of you confirmed believers. Aye and the most corrupt and polluted of you accepted and sanctified believers. No man ever became or long remained an infidel who did full justice to his Bible. And no believer but grew in grace and in strength and in holiness who constantly read his Bible, and who believed what he read in his Bible, and who honestly practised what he believed.

XXII

'THOU ART MY HIDING PLACE'

THE whole of the Bible is composed upon this proverb that man's extremity is God's opportunity. Adam and Eve hiding among the trees of the garden with all mankind hanging at their girdle, that gave God His great opportunity. Noah and his sons also, Abraham and Isaac, Jacob and Joseph, Moses and Aaron and Miriam, David and all the psalmists, Isaiah and all the prophets—it is all written to set forth man's extremity and to show forth God's opportunity. And when we come to the Son of Man Himself He is no exception to the universal rule. He is only the highest illustration and the most crowning fulfilment of this all-embracing proverb. For all through His life on earth His Father's Presence was His one Hiding Place also. But to come down to ourselves. The righteous wages of such a past life as yours and mine is our death; our death and all that ought to follow our death. And yet behold! we are

still alive and well and in the House of God to
hear what He has to say to us to-night about
our extremity and His opportunity.   Till we are
filled with wonder both at God and at ourselves
and till we exclaim with the wondering and en-
raptured prophet—Who is a God like unto Thee,
that pardoneth iniquity like mine, and passeth
by the transgression of a remnant like me ?   We
are exactly like Thomas Halyburton also one of
our own wondering prophets who writes this at
the close of the year 1797 : ' In all my exercises
about my great guilt my soul has always counted
all things but loss that it might win Christ and
more and more win to be found in Christ. When
fresh challenges disturbed, when thoughts of a
sudden summons to judgment were suggested,
whenever I was again in a strait, this was my
only sanctuary, to be found in Christ, not having
any righteousness of my own, nor seeking any
other righteousness but His.   For if this is
obtained I am safe, and nothing else but my
being found in him can ever make me think
myself safe.' Now if we obtain, like Halyburton,
to be found in Christ, we also, the worst of us,
are safe : as safe as Christ Himself is safe. Is not
that your mind, my brethren, as well as it was
the mind of Paul and Halyburton and Shepard ?
In putting their believing words into your mouth
am I overstating your case?   At any rate I am
not overstating my own case. And thus it is
that if you will not join with me I will make it
my own solo, as the music people would say, and

will sing alone to my God and Saviour, and will
say :

> Thou art *my* Hiding Place ; Thou shalt
> From trouble keep *me* free ;
> Thou with songs of deliverance
> About shalt compass *me* !

But before we go any farther let us ask as we
have been taught from our earliest years to ask
—Have all our transgressions of God's holy law
been equally heinous? No : by no manner of
means. For some sins in themselves, and by
reason of several aggravations, are far more
heinous in the sight of God and man than
others. As for instance, your past may be so
bad that in addition to the hurt you have done
to God and to His holy law there may be people
somewhere in your past life to whom you have
done a hurt far beyond any possible healing of
yours ; much as you would give and do to heal
and to restore them. There may be a man or a
woman or a child somewhere and sometime in
your past life of evil-doing to whom you have
done a damage beyond all possible reparation or
repair of yours. Some of them may be still alive
to keep you all your days in holy fear ; some of
them may be dead and in their own place to fill
your days and nights with the terror of the Lord.
Oh, man! Of all men the most miserable !
What a Cleft Rock you need to hide and to
shelter you ! Poor self-destroyed sinner how God
pities you in your awful extremity ! What an
opportunity God sees for Himself and for His

Son in you! And that is why He is sparing you
and is following you through all your miserable
life in such a gracious way. That also is why
He has led you up to this House of His to-night.
It was when Moses the man of God was in a
worse extremity than yours that God took His
greatest opportunity in all the Old Testament.
For it is written in Exodus and in letters of gold
that God descended and came and said to His
despairing servant, Behold, I have a Place by
Me, and I will put thee in a cleft of the Rock
which I have had opened for thee; and I will
cover thee with my own hand till all this sad
calamity of thine is wholly overpast. And it
was so. As often then as those injured and
angry ghosts rush in upon you out of your past
life do you with them like Moses. You know
what Moses did? He did this. He made haste,
and he bowed his head down to the earth, and
worshipped God who had condescended to come
to him in his terrible distress. Be you like Moses
in your terrible distress. Make haste and bow
your head and worship God. And He who is
able to save to the uttermost will take you as
His great opportunity to do that. You are the
uttermost man in all this house to-night and
therefore He is here to save and shelter you.
And more than that, where sin has so abounded
He will make His grace much more to abound,
till He will not seek and save you only, but in
answer to your unceasing prayer He will seek
and save those also whom you have hurt as only

He and you and they know or would believe.
And He will wipe all tears, not only from your
eyes, but better than that, from their eyes also
whose tears have been kept in His bottle against
you all these past impenitent years of yours.
' And they began to be merry,' says God's Son
about His Father's household. And in saying
that He means you; you and all who love you;
you and all they who have had such good cause
to hate you. Even all they whose merriment
you had for ever extinguished. Make haste then
like Moses; make haste like the prodigal son,
and see if the half has been told you about your
Father and about His great redemption which
He has had prepared for sinners like you.

Those of you who sing the psalms with any
spiritual understanding and with any personal
application must often have been arrested with
the way that all the prophets and all the psalmists
pray and importune about their shame. And
that not only about such shameful matters as the
matter of Uriah the Hittite, but about a multitude of matters concerning which nothing else is
told us but the resulting shame of them. ' My
confusion is continually before me, and the shame
of my face hath covered me,' sobs one of the sons
of Korah. ' O God,' cries David, ' Thou knowest
my foolishness, and my sins are not hid from
Thee.' And we understand and sympathise with
his extremity when he prays so importunately
and says: ' Let not them that wait on Thee be
put to shame for my sake. Let not them that

seek Thee be confounded for my sake, O God of
Israel.' And again: 'Thou hast known all my
shame and all my dishonour. Reproach hath
broken my heart, and for comforters I found
none.' And again, and this time in great assurance of faith : 'Thou shalt hide me in the secret
of Thy presence from the pride of men; Thou
shalt keep me secretly in a pavilion from the
strife of tongues.'

And then from all that the thing works itself
out in this way. When a man is brought to all
that then after that he not only hides himself
from all his past sin and shame, but he begins
now to hide himself from all his opportunities
and all his occasions of future sin. He watches
and prays now and henceforth against all the
times and against all the places and against
all the people that at one time he waited for
and welcomed. His constant prayer now is
that his feet and his eyes may be kept from
viewing vanity, and that God would guide him
and uphold him in His holy way. Aye, and
better than even that, his eyes are now opened to
see something of what a temptation and what a
snare he himself is in many ways to many other
men. And he hides himself, as much as may be,
from all men's eyes, and walks as softly and as in-
offensively as may be before all the weak and evil-
minded men about him. You understand? all
you that have received from God any such
humility of heart and any such spirituality of
mind.

I am afraid some of you will think that the whole life of a godly man is all hiding together. Yes, you are quite right; so it is. For there is this also. Every day the man of God and the disciple of Christ hides his daily cross in his great Hiding Place. And as he grows in this grace when he is again laid under his heaviest cross I will tell you what he does. He straightway washes his face from all his tears, and anoints his head from all the dust that he had heaped upon it, and he eats and drinks with you, and enters into all your merriment, till he completely deceives you about all his secret crosses; that is to say, unless you are yourself like him and thus see through him and all his hypocritical pretences. When our Lord was eating and drinking, and was conveying all kinds of comfort to His sorrowful disciples, all the time His broken heart was almost being torn out of His body, till He was compelled to leave His three most confidential disciples and seek a momentary hiding place with His Father among the olive trees of Gethsemane. Be like Him in that all of you who are numbered among His disciples. Go a good stone's cast away from your most intimate friends when your daily cross is being laid upon you heavier than ever. You understand? Yes, I am sure you do, all you who are taught of God and who are under His great sanctification.

And then to sum up for the present, far more close to you, and far more home-coming to you, and far more ever-present with you, than all your

other crosses and shames and temptations is the
cross and the shame and the temptation of yourself. Oh, what a life that miserable man lives
to whom he is his own constant cross! I cannot
attempt to describe to you his life, it is indescribable. It hath not entered into any other man's
heart to conceive it or believe it. No wonder
that God pities that man with all His pity. No
wonder that God saves that man with all His
salvation. No wonder that God comes down His
very self to be that man's inward comforter. For
God doth know, nay, there is nothing in all God's
knowledge that He knows so well as that chosen
man's inward agony. His inward sin, his inward
shame, his inward temptation, his inward cross.
No mortal man will ever know what some of their
fellow-men are passing through in their inward
Gethsemane and their inward Calvary. No
mortal man but that both mortal and immortal
Man the Man Christ Jesus. He alone knows us
and we alone know Him. And we openly avow it
and openly acknowledge it before God and before
all men and all angels, that we count it up as
well worth a thousand years of such indwelling
sin to come thereby to know somewhat of the
God-Man Christ Jesus. Yes; ten thousand
years of Paul's inward sin and Luther's inward
sin and Shepard's inward sin, if only it ends in
our increasing knowledge of Jesus Christ, in the
power of His resurrection, and in the fellowship
of His sufferings, and in our conformity to His
death. Let us go on then in the only way to

know Him. Let us go on into this new year more
and more to know Him, whom to know is eternal
life already. Let us enter on this new year, as
Paul entered on his Gospel preaching at Corinth,
determined to know nothing all this year compared with Jesus Christ, and Him crucified, and
ourselves crucified in Him and with Him. Let
us go to Him in our weakest hours, in our lone-
liest hours, in our most tempted hours, in our
most sin-dominioned hours, and in our most sin-
polluted hours. For to whom at such times can
we go but to Him; to Him who will never and
in no wise cast us out. And then from that let
us all this year go on like David our forerunner
to compass Christ about with songs of deliverance; ourselves and Him. With such songs of
deliverance as David's thirty-second Psalm, and
his fifty-first Psalm, and his hundred and third
Psalm, and his hundred and thirtieth Psalm.
And with such new songs of deliverance as
' 'Twas on that night,' and ' Hark the glad
sound,' and ' Jesus! how glorious is Thy grace,'
and ' Let troubles rise and terrors frown,' and
' Worthy the Lamb that died, they cry,' and
' Lo! these are they from sufferings great.' And
to crown it all and to make it all our own :

> Rock of Ages, cleft for *me*,
> Let *me* hide myself in Thee ;
> When I soar through tracts unknown,
> See Thee on Thy judgment throne,
> Rock of Ages, cleft for *me*,
> Let *me* hide myself in Thee.'

XXIII

'SOME REMORSES OF AN OLD MINISTER'

OUR old ministers have all the remorses of other men, but in addition to that they have many remorses of their own that other men know nothing about. No man lives to old age who has not a multitude of things in his past life that cause him keen remorse unless his conscience is seared with a hot iron. But our old ministers have a whole world of remorses that no other men, and happy for them, know anything about, and will not easily understand even when they are told them. At the same time I do not think it will be an ill-spent half-hour to-night if I tell you some of the remorseful experiences of one of the most faithful and most successful ministers that ever lived. The narrative may serve to open your eyes to some of the remorses and repentances and reformations that are going on in your own ministers, young and old, every day they live. 'Now, I beseech you,' said the Apostle, 'for the Lord Jesus Christ's

sake, and for the love of the Spirit, that ye
strive together with me, in your prayers to God
for me, lest that by any means when I have
preached to others, I myself should be a castaway.'

It was Thomas Shepard's oldest remorse in life
that he had been so long in making up his mind
to be a minister; to be one of the ministers of
Jesus Christ and a preacher of the everlasting
Gospel to the men of his own generation in
England. Shepard was born, so he tells us, in
an English town that was a perfect Sodom and
Gomorrah; a perfect sink of all sensuality and
profanity; and it was his lifelong wonder and
praise that he was dug out of such a ditch
and was sent to Cambridge to study for the
Christian ministry. Dr. Thomas Goodwin the
famous Puritan was preaching in Cambridge in
Shepard's undergraduate days and I can well
believe all that Shepard says of the unparalleled
power of Goodwin's pulpit work. At the same
time such was the hold that original sin had in
the young student's heart that he sums up his
first two years in Cambridge in these remorseful
words: an 'utter neglect of God, and an un-
conquerable aversion to secret prayer.' But
Goodwin's preaching gradually got such a hold
of young Shepard's conscience that it ultimately
ended in his complete conversion. Still, such
was the remaining worldliness and disloyalty of
his heart that he hesitated for a long time
before he finally gave himself up to the labours

and the dangers of the evangelical pulpit in that day of such atrocious oppression and persecution. The utter ungodliness of his student days and then his shameful slackness in surrendering himself to the service of his Saviour, these two memories of his youth caused Shepard deep shame and keen remorse all his after days. 'Despise not the ministry,' said Goodwin one Sabbath day in a sermon to students. 'The wares that the ministry deals in are immortal souls. No; despise not the ministry. God Himself had only one Son and He made Him a minister.' And that sermon both awakened a lifelong remorse in one hearer's heart, and at the same time sealed him to a lifelong service of the Son of God.

Not only had Shepard a lifelong remorse for his early unwillingness to enter the holy ministry, but added to that he had a lifelong remorse also on account of his great 'raw-headedness' after he was well on in his ministry. His early preaching when he looked back upon it was no preaching at all. It was everything but true preaching. And he himself was so far from being what a true preacher of the Gospel ought to be. And then the topics he preached on, and the way he preached on them, were neither the topics nor the treatment for which Jesus Christ had appointed the Christian pulpit. All that, when he looked back at it, made him see that he was an exact specimen of what John Bunyan in his own plain-spoken way calls 'a blundering and a raw-headed preacher.' 'When I began,' says Shepard, 'I neglected the great things of the Gospel; and I dwelt far too much on matters of but little moment. And I did not labour, as I ought to have laboured, to have the Holy Ghost seated in my heart when I was supposed to be delivering His message.' But the day came when all that so bitter remorse made Shepard a better and better preacher to the end of his life. Till this was the way he was spoken of in his funeral sermon and in the hearing of his broken-hearted people. 'He spent,' said the preacher, 'his whole week on his sermons. He finished his preparation for the Sabbath on Saturday afternoon; and then he gave up the whole evening to meditation and prayer. When he was dying he told the students assembled around his bed that every sermon he preached cost him both sweat and tears. He wrote his sermons out of his own heart, and thus it is that they still so reach the heart. They discover the sins, they satisfy the needs and they comfort the souls of all who hear and read them.' 'Who was wrought upon to-day?' was the usual question after a sermon of Shepard's; so did he preach, expecting an immediate result, and he got it. The exceeding sinfulness of sin, the exceeding greatness of salvation, and the exceeding glory of Christ were now his constant themes, as if to make up for the 'raw-headedness' of his early preaching. We have a thousand such testimonies to the reformation that Shepard's lifelong remorse produced upon his old age preaching upon his pastorate and upon his personal and family religion.

Like all praying men Shepard's heart held a deep remorse for his restraint of prayer. It was not that he restrained preaching about prayer. He preached plenty about prayer. For some years of his ministry he preached about little else. Indeed he so scolded his people about prayer that some of his most prayerful people left his intemperate and unbalanced ministry. The friend at midnight, the importunate widow, the Pharisee and the publican, Matt. vi. 6, Matt. vii. 7, John xvi. 24, Rom. xii. 12, Eph. vi. 18, Col. iv. 2, 1 Thess. v. 17, 1 Pet. iv. 7, and so on; there were weeks and months and years when you could not have sat a single Sabbath under Shepard's pulpit that you would not have heard a most heart-moving and a most conscience-searching sermon on some such texts as these. But all the time—he does not indeed say that he wholly neglected private prayer himself—but he will tell you that all that time he never prayed as he preached; he never all that time prayed either for himself or for others as he ought to have done. Even when he was most importunate in his own behalf he was basely forgetful of his family of his people and of his best friends. So much so that when it came to bidding his congregation and his family and his other friends farewell how his heart failed him for his neglect of prayer in their behalf.

Every one of his great texts came back to his
heart on his deathbed with a deadly stab. Oh!
he cried, had I my ministry to begin again I would
say far less about prayer in the pulpit but I would
perform it far more in the closet. And as he
opened the apostle's wonderful prayers for his
people, Shepard would fall on his knees and would
exclaim: 'Oh, my own people! Oh, my own
mishandled people! Oh, my own soul-murdered
people!' And then he would rise from his knees
saying: 'Would God I could put my old head
on the young shoulders of my son! But no; that
cannot be. Like his father he must learn wisdom
out of his own bitter experiences. Only, I will
bequeath my little book to him in the hope that
it may help him to a better old age than his
father's has been.'

As the years went on Shepard's pastoral work
left many a sharp sting in his pastoral conscience.
I suppose there was not a harder working man or
minister than Thomas Shepard in the whole of
New England. Day and night, Sabbath and
Saturday, he was incessantly at his work. But
he was not always at his right work. He did not
distribute his time and his strength always wisely.
His biographers tell us that 'his repute was
greatest among the best of his people.' And if
truth be told the good man was tempted to pay
most pastoral visits to the houses where his appre-
ciation and his repute were the greatest. Still,
repute or no, civility or no, his people were his
people; so much so that he seldom heard of the

death of one of his people that he had not
remorseful stings of conscience because of his
neglect of them both in their life and in their
death.

You will have difficulty in believing such a
humbling thing as this about such a man. But
have we not heard it sung that ' the saints are
lowered that the world may rise '? And no
man in all that old world was more lowered,
in his own eyes at any rate, than was Thomas
Shepard, because of Mr. T. H., and his great
name among the New England people; his
great name and the way his well-written books
sold so far beyond Shepard's atrociously badly-
written books. Some of you will remember that
black Sabbath day when Shepard was lying ill at
home and when his wife came back from church
and talked all day like a fool about Mr. T. H.,
his sermon. Talked and talked like a born fool
till she made her husband's bed in hell that
Sabbath night. Shepard spent that whole night
in the same bed with Heman the saddest the
gloomiest and the most sinful of all the psalmists.
Till he was convinced before morning that Heman
must have had almost as bad a heart at David as
he had at Mr. T. H., his too talented neighbour.
Shepard had not as yet found out the true cure
for the disease of such a heart as his, the cure
that William Law found out and published a
hundred years after but not in time for Shepard's
sanctification. ' If you would enjoy the prosperity
and the success of any rival of yours,' says the

great author of the *Serious Call,* ' pray that his
prosperity may be made a real blessing to him
and his. And if you would joyfully endure beside
you the man who at present is such a snare and
such a cross to you pray continually for his well-
being in every way. And surrounded as you are
with such men, pray for them all and actually
without ceasing.' So far as I see, Thomas Shepard,
with all his spiritual genius, had not made that
epoch-making discovery for his own sanctification.
At any rate he seems never to have got entirely
over Mr. T. H., his famous sermons and his
successful books.

But at this point Shepard takes us back again
to his people. His remorses are never long away
or far away from his people. And this time his
keen remorse is for the way he could never keep
himself from talking to his people about one
another. If any of his people happened to offend
him or to vex him or to disappoint him in any
way, do what he could, bridle in his tongue all
he tried, his hot heart would break out in most
unwise and most unguarded speeches concerning
the offenders. And then the offenders were always
told what the minister had said till there was no
end of bad blood and a bad conscience between
him and them. And till we meet with this remorseful entry again and again in his humiliated
diary, this : ' I see that I should never speak
about any of my people to their neighbours. If
my heart is often hurt with some of them, and is
often sore against some of them, I see now that I

should all the more set a watch on the door of
my lips. I should not carry my hurt to any of
their neighbours but to Him only whom they
have hurt far more than they can ever hurt me.'
But as we read on we have reason to believe that
Shepard quite got over this bad habit of his
some time before he died.

I feel sure that long ere now you must be dead
tired of Shepard and his endless remorses. You
will say that you could not have believed that a
minister with such a great name as Shepard could
have been so near being a castaway. And, therefore, I will not burden you with any more of his
remorses to-night, not that I have exhausted
them but I have far exhausted your patience
with him and with them and with me. Now just
one word in closing this discourse. I wonder
would all that remorse in that most remorseful
manse in New England be all on one side?
What think you? Would there be entire peace
of conscience and complete self-approval among
all Shepard's people all this time? I do not read.
I do not know. I cannot say. You will know
better than I do. And what do you say? For
instance, what do you say about his 'raw-headed'
preaching? Would they all know that his preaching was raw-headed? Some of them would but
would they all? Perhaps some of Shepard's
hearers preferred that kind of preaching. I have
seen as much even in our own advanced and enlightened day. Only, that raw-headed and raw-
hearted preacher came to repent and to reform

and to turn from all his rawness to be the ripest
and the richest and the most spiritual preacher
in all New England. I wonder if his people all
turned with him? What do you think?

Then about prayer? The first houses that
were built in New England by the pilgrim fathers
all had a secret place for prayer. Does that
architectural and domestic arrangement still continue in America? I have not been there and I
do not remember that any of our visitors to the
States have reported to us upon that. But how
about yourselves? Have you any place in your
house to which you can retire on occasion to
pray? And do you keep any record of the
people who ask you to pray for them and who
live on believing that you do? And what
method do you employ in order to find time and
retirement for this great responsibility? Poor
Shepard had terrible remorses on his deathbed
about God's neglected mercy-seat and about his
own neglected family and friends. Will you have
entire peace of mind toward God in that respect
when you are on your deathbed? What do you
think?

And then how about your fault-finding and
censorious talking about one another and especially about your ministers? I was not fishing for
it but an old elder was led on to tell me only
last night that when his children began to grow
up their mother and he came to a distinct understanding with one another that they were never
to say one single word to the detriment of either

of their ministers in the hearing of their children. And he dwelt upon that and illustrated that in a way that greatly impressed me. You will remember how Shepard transgressed against his people in that respect.

So much then for some of the remorses and repentances and reformations of that old minister, Thomas Shepard, English Puritan, pilgrim father, and founder of Harvard.

XXIV

'WHEN I READ CHRIST PRAYS'

'IT is a matter merely accidental to the Word of God to be written,' says Richard Hooker in his famous *First Book*. That is to say it is not at all essential or necessary to the Word of God that it be written out with pen and ink. And as a matter of fact our Lord who was Himself the living Word of God never wrote a line for us to read. And neither did any of His disciples for fifty or sixty years after He had finished all He had to say to them and to us through them. It was solely and entirely by the spoken Word that the Gospel was spread abroad in apostolic days. It was by the spoken word alone that the apostolic Churches of Rome and Corinth and Galatia and Ephesus and Colosse and Philippi and Smyrna and Pergamos and Sardis and Philadelphia and Laodicea were all first founded, and then built up. And it has always been by the spoken Word that the greatest victories of the Gospel have everywhere been won.

While it is quite true that there was nothing but a spoken Gospel for the first half-century of the Christian Church yet as time went on and as Christian communities were multiplied, it was found to be expedient, and indeed necessary, that the apostolic Gospel should be set down in a written form in the shape of Epistles and Gospels. And this went on till the New Testament was produced, exactly as we now possess it. And in possessing which we ourselves are taken up and are set abreast of the eleven disciples and the twelve apostles themselves—if we believe and obey what we there read. In which case we have our Lord's own word for it that He is as much our Master and our great High Priest as if we had sat beside Him in the upper room when He lifted up His eyes to Heaven and offered for Himself and for the eleven this High Priestly prayer. Such is the immense significance and the supreme importance to us of this evening's text :—'Neither pray I for these eleven alone, but for all them also who shall believe on me through their word.'

Come then and let us look at some of their words in this light.

And let us take John first. John who lay on his Master's bosom that night and who as we believe saw into his Master's mind and heart deeper and truer than any other of the eleven. And take John's very first word to us about his Divine Master. 'In the beginning was the Word, and the Word was with God, and the

Word was God. All things were made by Him;
and without Him was not anything made that
was made.' These, my brethren, are the pro-
foundest words that ever were written. The
angels, we may well say, desire to look into these
wonderful words, but draw back baffled and
abashed. Nor has the plummet of any exegete
nor the pulpit of any preacher ever gone to the
bottom of those wonderful words of John concerning his Master. And yet we, the sinful sons
of men, are bold to receive and to believe these
unfathomable words about our Redeemer. Indeed, once He has become to us our own Redeemer
there is nothing too wonderful for our faith and
our love to receive concerning Him. When once
God the Father has revealed His Son in us there
is no other revelation concerning Him that we
are not fully prepared to believe and to embrace.
Yes, we adoringly believe that He was with God
and was God. And we adoringly believe, and
every day more and more rejoice to believe, that
'all things were made by Him, and that without
Him was not anything made that was made.'
And we more and more look at all created things
in that evangelical light. We subscribe with all
our mind and heart to the Psalmist's confession
of the same faith: 'By the word of the Lord
were the heavens made, and all the host of them
by the breath of His mouth.' And we set our
hand to the corresponding confession of the
Apostle: 'For by Him were all things created
that are in heaven, and that are in earth; all

things were created by Him, and for Him; and
He is before all things, and by Him all things
consist.'   And where these and all such things
are far too high for us to understand—at any
rate in this life—we will still subscribe to them
till we do better, even fall down and adore. Yes,
before God and man, we wholly believe in the
Divinity, and in the Eternity, and in the Creator-
ship of our Blessed Lord, and all that through
John's words and through the words of all the
other apostolic men.   And having begun to
believe in that way we come down through the
whole of John's glorious prologue, believing at
every verse of it, till we come to that amazing
verse which might well stagger the strongest
faith, that amazing verse which runs thus : ' And
the Word was made flesh, and dwelt among us,
and we beheld His glory, the glory as of the
Only Begotten of the Father, full of grace and
truth.' Yes we believe that also. We do indeed.
We believe that had God seen good to cast our
lot in the fulness of time and had we lived in
Galilee or Jerusalem we would have beheld His
glory with our own eyes till we men would have
washed His blessed feet and our believing and
godly and wealthy women would have been like
Joanna and Susanna, who ministered to Him and
to His disciples of their substance.

And then the Word being made flesh we bring
up our children to be believers like ourselves by
reading to them and reading with them what is
written in Matthew and in Luke concerning the

manger at Bethlehem, and then what is written
in Luke concerning the Word when He was
twelve years old in our earthly life. And then
all our carpenters surely are adoring believers as
they work with the axe and the hammer and
think to themselves about Joseph's workshop.
And as they think and say to themselves that
this is 'the work of God, that they believe on
Jesus Christ whom God hath sent.' And then
we go on to read about His baptism and we
believe it as if we had seen it. And then about
His temptations and we believe both the facts of
them and the lessons that are drawn out for our
comfort from them. And then all the words that
His disciples report Him to have spoken till we
are able to say to the four evangelists what the
men of Samaria said to the woman who met our
Lord at the well: 'Now, we believe not only
because of your words, for we have heard Him
ourselves, and know that this is indeed the
Christ, the Saviour of the world.' We have
heard such things as these, and we believe that
He spake them; such things as these. 'They
that be whole need not a physician, but they
that are sick. I came not to call the righteous,
but sinners to repentance. . . . Come unto Me,
all ye that labour and are heavy laden, and I will
give you rest. . . . Behold my mother and my
brethren! For whosoever shall do the will of
my Father which is in heaven, the same is my
brother, and sister, and mother. . . . O woman!
great is thy faith; be it unto thee even as thou

wilt. . . . I say not unto thee until seven times, but until seventy times seven. . . .' And we read and believe the parable of the lost sheep, and the parable of the prodigal son. . . . And, to come back to John, we read and believe all these things: ' Behold the Lamb of God which taketh away the sin of the world. . . . For God so loved the world, that He gave His only begotten Son, that whosoever believeth in Him should have everlasting life. . . . Whosoever drinketh of the water that I shall give him shall never thirst: but it shall be within him a well of water springing up into everlasting life. . . . I am that bread of life. He that cometh to me shall never hunger, and he that believeth on me shall never thirst. . . . In the last day, that great day of the feast, Jesus stood and cried, saying, If any man thirst, let him come to me, and drink. . . . I am the good shepherd: the good shepherd giveth his life for the sheep. . . . Jesus said unto Martha, I am the resurrection and the life. Believeth thou this? . . . I am the true vine, and my Father is the husbandman, and ye are the branches. . . . Those things have I spoken unto you, that my joy might remain in you, and that your joy might be full. . . . Neither pray I for these alone, but for them also which shall believe on me through their word. . . . ' And many other words truly did Jesus speak in the presence of His disciples, which are not written in this or in any book. But these and such like are written that ye might believe that Jesus is the Christ,

the Son of God, and that, believing, ye might
have life through His Name.

Now, my brethren, it was with us also in His
mind and in His heart that night that He said
concerning us these ever-blessed words which He
has put into our mouths for our text this evening,
—these ever-blessed words : 'Father, for them
also I pray who shall believe on me through their
word.' That is to say, the Son of God makes
prayer and intercession for us this day and at
this hour as truly as He made prayer and intercession for the eleven in that upper room that
passover night. That is to say, if not for all of
us, at any rate for as many of us as believe on
Him through such words of His disciples as our
ears have now heard. Come then all you who do
believe, come and listen to some of the petitions
that your great High Priest is offering for you at
this moment before the throne. For looking
down on you He points to you as He says to
His Father concerning you : 'And this is life
eternal, that they might know thee, the only
true God, and Jesus Christ, whom thou hast
sent. For I have given them the words which
thou gavest me, and they have received them,
and have known surely that I came out from
thee, and they have believed that thou didst
send me.' Now, would He be right if He said
that to His Father about you ? Have you known
surely that He came out from the Father and
came to you ? And have you believed that the
Father sent Him expressly and immediately to

you? If so, happy are you! The holiest angel around the throne envies you. And still He proceeds concerning you. 'And now I am no more in the world, but these—you and I—are in the world. I pray not that thou shouldest take them out of the world, but that thou shouldest keep them from the evil.' And, when your appointed time comes, and mine—'Father, I will also, that they whom thou hast given me be with me where I am; that the love wherewith thou hast loved me may be in them, and I in them.' O my brethren, my believing brethren! heard you ever such things as these? Such surpassingly glorious things as these? No, never! For 'ear hath not heard, nor eye seen, neither have entered into the heart of man the things which God hath prepared for them that love Him.'

Let us take one or two reflections and lessons out of all that before we shut their word and go home.

1. And first, reflect much on the great blessedness of having the disciples' words concerning their Master in your hands to read them when you please.

2. And then reflect much on the unspeakable blessedness here promised to all who believe. For such blessedness is there in believing that it makes you more blessed in this far-off house this evening than if you had been in the upper room that night with your names written among the eleven. Yes, I am not overstating your blessedness in saying that, for are not these your

Saviour's own spoken words concerning His disciples of that day, and concerning you His disciples of this day? Are not these His very words spoken by Him and written down for your faith? 'Thomas,' He said, 'because thou hast seen me thou hast believed : blessed are they that have not seen and yet have believed.' Better then to be reading the seventeenth of John in this house this evening than to have been in the upper room and heard it spoken that night, Better and more blessed to read this chapter in your chair at home this Sabbath night than to have leaned on His breast as He uttered it that passover night. Such is the supreme blessedness that is placed within the reach of all men who have the Four Gospels concerning Christ put into their hands.

3. And then this is surely by far the best reflection and lesson of all. There is the great joy you can give to Jesus Christ, even in glory, by your believing on Him through their word. For do you not hear the tone of true satisfaction, the tone of great gratification that sounds again and again through this whole High Priestly prayer of His? 'Thine they were,' He says to His Father concerning you—'Thine they were, and thou gavest them me, and they have kept thy word.' And again, 'For I have given unto them—pointing to you—the words which thou gavest me ; and they have received them, and have known surely that I came out from thee, and they have believed that thou didst send me.' And again,

' O Righteous Father, the world hath not known thee; but I have known thee, and these have known that thou hast sent me.' Yes, as many of you as believe on Him through their word, He sees in you of the travail of His soul, and is satisfied. Such true blessedness is there, both to Him and to you in your reading your New Testament and believing what you read. Let us then more and more search both the Gospels and the Epistles of the New Testament for in them we know that we have eternal life, and they are they that testify to us of our Great High Priest.

XXV

'SURELY I HAVE LAID MY PIPE FAR SHORT OF THE FOUNTAIN'

AS I was reading James Fraser of Brae the other night, and for the fiftieth time, as Dr. Jowett once said about his Boswell—I came again on this characteristic and suggestive passage. 'Surely,' he says, 'I have laid my pipe far short of the fountain, for I am as blind, and as dead, and as unholy as ever I was.' But as I read that I immediately remembered that Fraser had only borrowed both the figure and the fact of that from a great authority of his, even from our old friend Thomas Shepard of New England. And on looking up the parent passage, I found that these were Shepard's exact words: 'As it is with conduit pipes, so here,' he says. 'Let the pipes be laid ever so well, and laid ever so far up, yet if they are not laid wholly and all the way up to the conduit head, no water will ever come down to that family.'

Now these two passages from those two masters in Israel were enough for my self-examination that pre-communion night. And accordingly I laid down my two teachers and fell athinking to myself. 'A conduit-head,' 'a fountain-head,' thought I. 'A fountain-head, and a pipe running up, so far, toward that fountain-head.' And as I looked and looked at that and made a mental picture of that I said to myself—No! No city corporation anywhere ever did such a stupid thing as that. No town council in all the land ever took the city taxes and ran a pipe half-way, or three-fourths of the way, up to a lake of sweet water in the far-off hills. And no house-holder was ever so insane as to have a fine spring rising in his high grounds and then to run a conduit pipe a certain way up in the direction of that spring and then to let the water take its chance of finding its way into the unfinished pipe and so its chance of ever watering his house and his garden and his grounds. No man out of an asylum ever perpetrated an act of insanity like that. No man but you and I. Only you and I are so far left to ourselves as to do a thing like that, and that only in the matter of our religion, in the supreme matter of the salvation of our own souls and the souls of our households. And as I sat alone with my own thoughts a succession of scenes and circumstances and instances arose before my eyes, some of which I shall now try to put before you for your profit, if you will attend to them.

'With Thee,' sings the Psalmist in a fine psalm —'With Thee is the fountain of life.' Of all

life, that is. For all life everywhere and of all
kinds has its first fountain in God. All life, and
of all kinds. But it is of the very Divine life
itself that David here sings. And this great
thing begins for us New Testament men in this
wonderful and adorable way. When our Lord
Himself was still down here, in this same thirsty
land, He also ran His pipe up to the Divine
fountain. As often as He felt athirst, or felt
that He needed more life and more strength and
more solace than He had in Himself, He again
ran His pipe of prayer and of faith and of Sonship trust up to His Father in Heaven. He tells
us that in some of His greatest sermons. And
He lets us see Himself doing that in such wonderful words as these : ' As the Father hath life in
Himself, so hath He given to the Son to have
life in Himself.' And again : ' As the living
Father hath sent me, and I live by the Father,
even so He that eateth me, he shall live by me.'
In these wonderful words the Son of God offers
Himself to us as a sort of subordinate and second
Fountain, so to speak, up to which we are told
to run the pipe of our faith and of all our spiritual
life. And again : ' Because I live,' he says, ' ye
shall live also.' And thus it was that He was
able to say to the thirsty woman at the well of
Samaria, ' Whosoever drinketh of the water of
this well shall thirst again, but whosoever drinketh
of the water that I shall give him, it shall be in
him a well of water springing up into everlasting
life.' And then He has had it written concern-

ing Himself on the last page of our New Testament : ' I am Alpha and Omega, the first and the last. And I will give to Him that is athirst of the water of life freely. And the Spirit and the Bride say come. And let him that heareth say come. And let him that is athirst come. And whosoever will, let him come and take of the water of life freely.' The Son of God is set before us in these and in many more Scriptures as so to speak a second, and as so to speak a much nearer Fountain, bringing down the water of life toward us and inviting us to run up our pipe to Him. There is a beneficent law of nature which is but a parable of a still more beneficent law of grace. And that beneficent and blessed law of grace is that the water of life rises in the Son as high as its first source in the Father. And it stands in all its fulness in the Son for us to draw it from Him. ' And,' says one, speaking in this respect for all believers— ' And of His fulness have all we received, and grace for grace.'

Now all that being so ; the Father of all being the First Fountain of all life and all blessedness, and the Son being as it were the still nearer and the more accessible Fountain of the same life and the same blessedness, how do we do and how ought we to do in this matter of running our pipe up to Christ, and thus receiving continually out of His fulness ?

In the great waterworks of New Testament times the aqueduct-builders erected great arches

and great bridges and great piers and great pillars
on which they laid the great stone channels which
were intended to carry the water from the far-off
hills to the thirsty cities. But in all my ancient
reading I never once read of any Roman architect
who ever ran his aqueduct up to this arch or to
that pier or to that pillar and then left it standing there unfinished and utterly useless. Had any
ill-intended or incompetent architect ever done
such a criminal thing as that he would have been
beheaded for his folly and for his cruelty to the
parched people who had employed him. But
what we never read of having once happened in
all the Roman Empire, that is what we ourselves
do every day in the Church of Christ. We run
our pipe up so far in the direction of the living
water. But for the most part we leave our pipe
hanging idly in mid-air and wholly empty of the
living water for the want of which we and our
household are all dying of thirst. And thus it
is that, as Fraser says, ' After we have done all
we are as blind, and as dead, and as unholy as
ever we were.' As Shepard says, ' No water ever
comes down to that family.' For to come to instances and to examples, what is the very Bible
itself but a high and a heavenward arch on which
we are told to rest the pipe of our faith as we run
our faith up to Him whose word of life our Bible
is? And so is it with the pulpit. For what is
the most evangelical pulpit when it is at its very
best but another pier and pillar up to which we
run our pipe, and thus pass above and beyond

the pulpit to Him who built it for our faith to rest on it so as to rise above it? And so is the very mercy-seat itself. We too often make our prayers an end and an object in themselves. We too often bow down before the throne of grace and rise up and come away without having once lifted up our hearts to Him who sits upon that throne. As Fraser says in another place, 'We say our prayers, indeed, but we seldom ask ourselves whether we have had an audience of the heavenly king or no.' We run our pipe on occasion up to all these great means of grace but we stop short at the means and we seldom if ever come close up to Him who has all the grace in Himself, and who waits to be gracious to all those who come up to His presence for His grace. And so it is with the Sabbath and with the Lord's Supper itself. The Sabbath and the Supper are but another two additional arches and bridges and piers and pillars built for 'our spiritual nourishment and growth in grace,' by our Heavenly Architect. And on which He intends us to lay our pipes up and up and up to Himself, the Heavenly Fountain of all grace and all truth, and all eternal life. 'I secretly rested,' confesses Fraser, 'on the act of faith, and did not rise, as I ought to have risen, to the Object of faith. I drew my life, and my strength, and my comfort more from my own believing than from Him on whom I believed.'

My brethren, you all see the situation, do you not? You all take to yourselves the reproof and the correction, do you not? You all read your-

selves the lesson, do you not? And you resolve
to be more sane, and more wise, and more merciful to yourselves in the future, do you not? and
this very week, and this very communion season?
That is to say, you will all this week of preparation run your pipe of repentance, and of prayer,
and of faith, and of newness of life, not up to the
penitential psalms only, nor up to pre-communion
pulpit only, nor up to the Lord's table only, but
the whole way up to Him toward whom all these
piers and pillars but help to lift you. Ever up
and up and still up to Jesus Christ himself, the
only true and sure and sufficient Fountain of all
your salvation.

Yes, let us all begin aright and at once with
our repentance and all the rest will follow—every
other communion-week grace in its evangelical
order. Let us begin with a deep and a true
repentance. But let us look well to it that our
repentance does not terminate upon ourselves.
Let us not content ourselves with 'coming to ourselves,' like the prodigal son in the parable. Let
us be like him in that. But let us go on to be
like him in this also, that he came back to his
father. 'They return,' complained the prophet
concerning repentant Israel, 'they return, but
not to the Most High.' Let us all return, and
at this season, all the way to the Most High.
When we sing, as we every day shall sing, 'There
is a fountain filled with blood,' let us look at the
blood as it is flowing down upon us every day
from Immanuel's veins. And as we sing and sob

and sink out of sight in that fountain opened for all our sins and for our uncleanness, let us all the time rise above the fountain and ascend up to Him, in whose sin-atoning blood that fountain is opened and is kept opened. Let us come up close to the Cross and to Christ Himself dying upon the Cross and say to Him with William Cowper:

> Dear dying Lamb ! Thy precious blood
> Shall never lose its power !

And so on through all the soul-saving and God-glorifying exercises of the communion season; through all its private and public privileges; through all its reading and meditation at home; through all its preaching and all its hearing in the preparation services; and then through all our partaking of the Body and Blood of the Son of God at His table. Let us in all and always run our pipe up to the Fountain, even to the Son of God, our Saviour. For with Him is the Fountain of Life.